E. Lynn ("Fox") and Chuck Morton
Second Edition
Revised by E. Lynn ("Fox") Morton

Ferrets

Everything about Purchase, Care, Nutrition,
Diseases, Behavior, and Breeding

With 41 Color Photographs;
Illustrations by Michele Earle-Bridges

Consulting Editor: Matthew M. Vriends, Ph.D.

BARRON'S

Contents

Before acquiring a ferret—no matter how cute it appears—be sure that you are prepared to give it the attention it needs.

Preface

We encountered our first ferret in a pet store many years ago and my husband fell in love. I, on the other hand, was reluctant. Was it a wild animal? Did it bite? What did it eat? Would it play? Did it like other animals—our five dogs in particular? Could it be litter trained? And most important— would it love us back? Unfortunately, the store clerk knew only that it was sweet, docile, and playful. My caution prevailed and we left without the slinky, furry creature.

My husband does not give up easily. We acquired books—there aren't nearly enough. We visited pet stores. We traveled to several small breeders' homes. We corresponded with people at a university that maintains a breeding colony. Finally, we brought home our first 10 ferrets.

These 10 delightful creatures accomplished what the books and talk had not been able to do—they completely captured my heart too. A sable female named Crystal was to become our constant companion. Traveling to town riding in the hood of my husband's coat, sleeping peacefully in my lap, begging for red licorice (her favorite), shuffling along under our feet, and playing with wild abandon— she was everything you could ask for in a companion. It hardly seems possible to pack so much personality into such a small body.

Over the next year we bred our ferrets, cared for them and their young, and agonized over the inadequacy of our knowledge. Gradually, we learned more. We continued to run up tremendous phone bills looking for information.

We then added a breeding colony of about 75 animals. Once again we were confronted with the lack of available knowledge. Surely our neighbors must have mountains of cages. We discarded cage after cage, system after system, until we found one that worked—housing in which the ferrets could be comfortable, happy, and productive.

Our expanded ferret family grew. We added males, when available, of a suitable temperament, conformation, and markings. We wanted productive mothers, but that was just the beginning. Docile temperament, wide catlike heads, and good markings are of great importance. The average size of the ferrets bred in the U.S. has increased by about 20 percent over the years. I guess my preference for larger ferrets shows up in the breeding program. We felt the acquisition of new males was important so the colony would not become inbred and lose the vigorous good health natural to a ferret. Our ferret colony has grown quite large now. The babies are all loved, handled, tickled, kissed, and played with by both us and the teenage gentlers here.

Ferrets are still misunderstood. The myths abound. No—ferrets are not wild animals. They are domestic—just like cats and dogs. There are no "wild" ferrets. Ferrets cannot survive without your continued care and support. No they do not establish in the wild. Yes—the female really can die if left in heat during the entire breeding season. She must be spayed or kept continually bred. No—ferrets don't use their scent glands against you like skunks. They have anal sacs, but so do dogs.

In this book we have incorporated the knowledge gained from years of experience, as well as information gained from articles, veterinarians, and books. We hope that this book will help you better care for, understand, and enjoy your ferret. Given a good under-standing and knowledge of them, you will find ferrets truly delightful animals. We cannot imagine being without ferrets, and yet they are not for everyone. Ferrets are social animals and they require a commitment from you. Their temperament is roughly midway between that of a dog and a cat. They are not as dependent as dogs, but they are more dependent than cats. We wish you much fun with your ferrets and yes—they truly do love you back.

Fox Morton
Spring, 1985

Preface to the Second Edition

Due to the many strides forward in ferret health issues, we here at Path Valley Farm felt it was essential to get the latest information into the hands of those of you who own or are owned by one or more ferrets.

• Nearly all ferrets are now neutered and de-scented *before* being sold. This is done to protect the ferret from health risks.

• There is an *approved* rabies vaccine for ferrets.

• Although there are still a few states where ferrets are unwelcome, the majority of states where ferrets were not allowed have now changed their regulations.

• There are a number of good ferret foods on the market.

• There are now texts for veterinarians who wish to study ferrets. There are also many good articles detailing ferret health issues (see page 70).

I am grateful to Matthew M. Vriends, Ph.D. and Fredric L. Frye, D.V.M. for many suggestions that have improved this book.

Fox Morton
Spring, 1995

Is a Ferret Right for You?

Adding a new family member is an important decision—a decision that should never be made on impulse no matter how adorable the soft furry kits (babies) are. You must be prepared to make a time commitment to any new animal. In all fairness to the ferret, stop and consider these points.

• A ferret will require care. You must make sure it has fresh food and water. Its cage must be cleaned and its litter changed as needed. Can you do this without resenting the animal?

• Are you prepared to spend the time required getting acquainted with the new baby? If this is a very busy time in your life, would it be better to postpone the decision?

• If you rent your apartment or house, have you checked to be sure you will be allowed to keep a ferret?

• What will you do when vacation time comes? Is there room in the car for a cage, or is there someone who can care for your ferret while you are away?

• Ferrets require neutering (spaying in females and castration in males) to be good, healthy pets. Female ferrets often die from aplastic anemia if they are not neutered. Male ferrets can become overly aggressive if not neutered. Ferrets sold by reputable stores and breeders usually will have already had this surgery performed to protect the ferret. Is there somewhere near you where you can obtain this type ferret or are you prepared for the surgical expense on an unaltered ferret?

• Ferrets should be de-scented—preferably *before* you purchase your pet—to reduce their odor and to eliminate any future risk of infected or blocked scent glands. The majority of the ferrets sold today will have already had this operation completed. If you are not able to find a ferret that was de-scented before purchase, can you find a veterinarian who routinely does this surgery? Are you willing to incur this expense?

• If the ferret is to belong to your child is he or she really willing to love and care for the pet daily? Next year too?

• Ferrets require one of the special ferret foods now on the market or, at a minimum, a high-quality dry cat food. Will this be a burden to your budget?

• Kits can be overzealous in their play and nip too hard. Could you scold and discipline your kit or would it be easier to "let it go"? Consistent discipline is part of loving the animal in a responsible manner.

• The ferret will live for 8 to 11 years. Are you prepared for a long-term commitment?

• Babies or young children should not be left unsupervised with any pets. This includes ferrets. This is for the safety of both the ferret and the child. The child could accidentally harm such a small pet. The ferret, even though it is tiny, has sharp teeth like a puppy or kitten and should be supervised by an adult.

• Do you have pets in the rodent family? If so, you must keep in mind that ferrets are mousers. The other pet must be kept in a safe environment.

Considerations Before You Buy

Once you have decided that a ferret is right for you, you should make a few preliminary decisions before you purchase a pet. Do you want a male or a female? One ferret or two? Do you want a baby kit or an adult? You must also be sure that you purchase a healthy animal from a reputable dealer.

Male or Female?

Choosing the color and sex of your new ferret is strictly a matter of personal preference. Males and females require about the same amount of space and time. Both are equally hardy. The sexes do not differ greatly in behavior; ferrets have individual personalities. A particular color or sex does not influence the nature of the pet.

Male and female kits start out at about the same size. However, the mature male is about twice the size of the mature female. Males will range from 3 to 5 pounds (1.5–2.5 kg), while females grow to a mere 1½ to 3 pounds (0.75–1.5 kg).

Neutered and de-scented ferrets have very little odor, but a spayed and de-scented female has the least odor of all. After all, you have only half as many pounds of ferret in the house.

Females must be spayed unless repeatedly bred at each heat; otherwise, they frequently develop a serious disease called aplastic anemia and die. The cost of spaying should be considered before acquiring a female. (Obviously, the cost of neutering a male ferret must also be considered if you are unable to obtain one that has been altered and de-scented.)

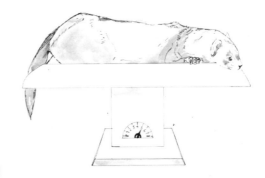

Mature male ferrets are larger than females, ranging from about 3 to 5 pounds (1.5–2.5 kg).

My tip: As previously mentioned, the majority of the animals sold today will have been de-scented and neutered. However, it is wise to ask the breeder or pet store dealer about both operations before completing your purchase.

Mature female ferrets seldom grow to more than 3 pounds (1.5 kg).

Which Color?

There are a number of colors now being bred: sable (the most common color), red-eyed white, silver-mitt, sterling silver, white-footed sable. butterscotch, white-footed butterscotch, and the rare and beautiful cinnamon ferret.

Sable: Marked and masked like raccoons, it's easy to understand their popularity. Sables range widely from light to dark, depending on the shade of both the underfur and guard hairs. The underfur ranges from white to beige. This fur will sometimes have a slight golden cast to it. The guard hairs are longer and are black. A well-marked sable ferret should have a definite mask or hood pattern over the face. The preferred nose color is black to match the "trim." The face should be short and broad.

Red-eyed White: This color is frequently referred to as albino. Red-eyed whites range in color from white to golden; some are albinos and some are not. It is only through breeding that this can be determined. We actually have a male who is a red-eyed white and has one section of black hair just over his tail. Noses are, of course, pink. It is especially important in the whites for the animal to have a short, broad head. A ferret should in no way resemble a rat.

Silver-mitt: The underfur of the silver-mitt is white or off-white. The guard hair contains both black and white strands. This mix is what accounts for the silvery appearance. A silver-mitt ferret will also have four white feet and a white bib. The eyes appear black but are frequently a deep burgundy.

Sterling Silver: The sterling silver ferret is marked like the silver-mitt. The difference is in the ratio of black to white guard hairs: the sterling silver has considerably more white strands in the guard hair, thus giving it a much paler appearance than the regular medium silver shade.

White-footed Sable: This ferret is marked like a standard sable ferret but has four white feet and a white throat patch. They do not all show the throat patch characteristic. The white-footed sables do not have white guard hairs as do the silvers. Noses are generally black.

Butterscotch: The underfur of the butterscotch ferret is the same as that of the sable. However, the guard hairs, leggings, and mask or hood patterns are butterscotch rather than black. Noses are generally butterscotch to match the guards.

White-footed Butterscotch: This color is still relatively rare. Marked like a butterscotch, this ferret has the four white feet and white throat patch of the silver-mitts.

Cinnamon: Truly beautiful, this color is still rare. The underfur is white or off-white. The guard hair is the rich red-brown color of cinnamon.

Black-eyed Whites: This is a color that ferret breeders have been trying to obtain for years. This is still a relatively rare color, but it is now possible to obtain black-eyed whites as pets.

Spotted: A few spotted ferrets are seen each year. Spotting most often appears on the stomach but occasionally also covers the back. The back pattern generally disappears with the adult coat. Spotted kits often have "possum-looking" marking on their faces. We now see spotted adults with white bodies and a striking splash of black at the back of one leg. These are very rare.

Ferrets come in a variety of colors. Top: male sable (left) and female cinnamon (right). Center: female butterscotch (left) and female sterling silver (right). Bottom: male ecu sable (left) and female black-eyed white (right).

What Age?

A well cared for ferret generally lives from 8 to 11 years. In selecting a pet there are advantages and disadvantages to kits and adults.

A kit can be a great source of joy to raise and train. If you are new to ferrets, kits are less intimidating because they are so tiny. On the other hand, kits require more time to train. They need consistent discipline for housebreaking and for avoiding too-rough play. They can also be rowdy adolescents before becoming settled adults.

Adult ferrets—if they have been well handled—are past all these stages. However, adults who have not been handled with love and discipline are poor choices and are best left to experts. A grown ferret has the ability to adapt to and love the new family quickly. After only a short time, you will be amazed at how easily the adult becomes a member of the family. Perhaps it will already be litter or cage trained. If not, it can still learn and be disciplined. Another advantage with an adult is that you can see the animal's exact size, coat color, and marking pattern. As with the kit, it is usually less expensive to purchase an adult that has already been neutered and de-scented. If the adult has not been altered, be sure to check with your veterinarian regarding the cost of surgery before purchasing your ferret.

The final decision comes down to which ferret you find and fall in love with. If it is a kit, you'll have a great learning experience together. If it is an adult, it will quickly learn to love you as if you had raised it yourself.

One Ferret, a Pair, or a Group?

Ferrets are social animals. One ferret, given some play time and toys, will entertain itself and you quite successfully. If possible, place the animal's housing near an activity-oriented section of your home such as the kitchen, living room, or dining area. Because ferrets are so active, they sleep up to 14 hours per day. If there is nothing interesting to do, ferrets tend to catch some shut-eye; thus, the ferret is ready to play and explore when you have the time. Ferrets are frequently caged for their own safety at night or while everyone is away. You should allow them some freedom to explore and play out of the cage under supervision during at least part of your at-home time. If you already have a dog or cat, the ferret will soon teach them some ferret games.

If you are contemplating buying a pair of ferrets, you should know that they need not be purchased together. An adult ferret will—after a very short adjustment period—accept another adult or a kit. If you have very little time for your pets, a pair of ferrets will keep each other company. They will, however, still want some freedom and a chance to include you in their games. The fun of watching two ferrets roll and tumble together more than compensates for the additional work. They prefer to live in the same cage and can use the same bowls.

A word of caution: Unneutered males should not be housed with other ferrets. They become so territorial during breeding season that serious injury or death for the other ferret can result.

Groups of ferrets are as much fun as a circus. We know a young couple who has converted their spare bedroom to a ferret playground. There are slides and sandboxes. Tubes made from a 4-inch (10-cm) plastic drainage pipe were used to create a giant tunnel system. An old handbag suspended on a rope and spring created a swing that bounced up and down. There are crinkly bags for the ferrets to jump on and crawl into and out of. There is even a remote control car for the ferrets to chase and capture. This couple says, "It's more fun to have

friends over to watch the ferrets than to go to the movies."

Neutered, De-scented, or Both?

Neutered and de-scented kits are available nearly anywhere in this country now. They are an excellent choice. If you are unable to find a neutered and de-scented ferret, you will want to have this surgery done as early as possible. Be sure to check with your veterinarian concerning the cost of these surgeries before you purchase a ferret that is not already neutered and de-scented.

If you purchase an unneutered ferret, your sweet baby will begin to smell and secrete so much musk he will become greasy to the touch during breeding season. Unless you plan on keeping him and starting a serious breeding farm, you will want to attend to this early on and avoid this unpleasant situation.

Even a grown, smelly male can be neutered and de-scented and will regain his desirability as a cuddly pet—but it takes about 30 days for musk secretions to stop. Moreover, the aggression level of unneutered males becomes high enough to require them to be housed separately.

Female ferrets, under natural lighting conditions and kept outside, come into heat about February and remain in heat through September (they do *not* cycle in and out of heat during this period like most mammals). This prolonged heat cycle and its concurrent high levels of estrogen lead to aplastic anemia and septicemia. This condition can cause about 90 percent of all females left unbred to die during their first spring-summer after birth. Unless the female is to be kept as a breeder, *she must be spayed.* De-scenting at this time is a good idea for odor control and to eliminate any possible health risks from infected scent glands. Many veterinarians prefer to perform this de-scent surgery at the same time they spay or castrate a ferret.

Ferrets have anal scent glands. Like skunks, which have a special adaptation enabling them to use their glands as an offensive weapon, ferrets can expel an unpleasant odor, but do so only in fear of their life, e.g., during rough handling or play with other ferrets that gets out of hand. This ferret spray, however, is not to be confused with skunk spray. Ferret

Ferrets are social animals. They enjoy playing with one another and with toys like a ball.

spray dispels in an average room within minutes and washes off easily with soap and water.

The decision to de-scent is a personal one for pet owners, but it should definitely be done when plugged scent glands are a recurrent problem. Evidence indicates that de-scenting does lower the odor level of males and females.

My tip: It is safest to purchase a ferret that is already neutered and de-scented. Then, you will not face these risks for your pet.

Where to Purchase a Ferret

No matter where you purchase your pet, the most important element is the knowledge of the seller. In your first experience with an unfamiliar animal, you will have many questions. An experienced seller can allay unfounded fears and help handle any real problems you may encounter—from health to training to tricks.

The two most common sources of pet ferrets are pet stores and small local breeders.

From a Pet Store

In most areas, there is an abundance of pet stores. You can find them through ads in your phone book and newspapers and by recommendations of friends.

A well-recommended pet shop should be your first choice for shopping for a ferret. You should also visit as many stores as you can. You should compare quality carefully. A low price can never make up for a poor-quality ferret with health or behavior problems. You should be able to obtain a ferret that is already neutered and de-scented. The ferret should be both playful and docile in temperament.

A clean, well-lighted, and well-run pet store is a real treat for all animal lovers. The excitement of seeing all the animals, plus a wide selection of items for your pet, makes for a worthwhile visit.

Unfortunately, some stores do not meet these expectations. A few owners allow their stores to become a motley collection of ill-kept animals. However, the

Ferrets getting to know one another: a white female and a sable male.

majority of pet stores do provide the best possible animals and supplies.

Here is what to look for in a good pet shop:
- All animals should appear healthy, be active when appropriate, and be in suitable enclosures.
- All areas and enclosures should be clean and odor-free.
- Feeding and watering equipment should be clean and algae-free.
- A wide selection of food, simple medicines, toys, cages, and training equipment for each species should be available.
- Lighting should be suitable for each species.
- The staff should be clean and well-groomed.
- A selection of books about animals should be available.
- The pet shop owner and the employees should be willing to gather information and make it available to you
- The shop should have a good reputation with other customers and with local business groups. A phone call to these references is time well spent before making a major purchase.

Remember that, because of the order of jobs to be done, not all these factors are possible at every moment of the day. After all, some cages must be cleaned first and some last.

However, over the course of several visits you should not see any single area neglected. Such neglect is a good reason to avoid the store.

From a Local Breeder

Local breeders can be found through their ads in newspapers under the column for pets, and in small direct ad papers. When visiting a small breeder, remember the following do's and don'ts.
- **Do** call ahead for an appointment. This saves wasted trips and ensures you that the breeder will have the time available to help you select a pet and provide you with the information you need.
- **Do** ask to see the parents of the kits. The personality, size, and temperament of the parents are reflected in their offspring.
- **Do** ask to see a selection, if possible. A group of ferrets playing will tell you about the behavior of the individual kits.
- **Do** ask if the ferret has already been neutered and de-scented. If not, ask about veterinarians in the area who do these operations, and check on the cost.
- **Do** observe the general condition of the facility. A clean, well-kept breeding area indicates that the breeder cares for the animals and that your kit will be well started toward good health.

A pair of ferrets will keep each other company—and you will enjoy watching them play together.

- **Do** ask lots of questions. How long has the breeder been breeding ferrets? How many animals are there? What are the names and phone numbers of other customers?
- **Don't** take other animals along. Other pets may bring fleas, colds, and other germs to the breeding colony.
- **Don't** take people with colds or other infectious illnesses with you.
- **Don't** let children under six years of age play with animals they don't know.
- **Don't** buy on impulse, no matter how cute the kits are.

An active, intelligent animal who lives from 8 to 11 years should be a well-thought out purchase.

Any reputable breeder should have knowledge and in-depth experience with ferrets of all ages and offer personal service and advice on keeping ferrets. Unfortunately, there are many breeders who do not meet these high standards, Do check carefully before choosing a breeder.

Signs of Health to Look For When Buying

In selecting your ferret, you should look for the following:

1. Bright, clear eyes of even size. Some ferrets suffer from very small eyes (microphthalmia). Secretions of any kind indicate infection or irritation.

2. Long full whiskers. Short broken whiskers indicate poor nutrition and sometimes infections.

3. No large lumps on the body. These lumps may be cancerous.

4. A soft full coat. The guard or long hairs should be firm enough to stand out from the soft wool of the undercoat.

5. Firm and even distribution of muscle. The ferret should appear long, muscular, and athletic as an adult. Healthy kits have large, full bellies.

6. Clean genital areas. Feces around the anal area indicate diarrhea, and secretions around the vulva or penis are signs of genitourinary infections.

7. Good temperament and attitude. The prospective pet should be playful and gentle. Play biting and mock combat are a normal occurrence. Painful bites or overly aggressive attitudes should be avoided.

8. Curiosity. A socialized kit should have no fear of new people, objects, or sounds. A confident attitude is the mark of a healthy and happy ferret.

Expenses of Purchase and Maintenance

The average retail price of a neutered and de-scented ferret in pet stores is about $150. The more unusual colors sometimes cost somewhat more. (If you are considering an animal that is not yet neutered and de-scented, check on the cost of these surgeries in your area.) The purchase price is much less than that for other animals of similar intelligence and life span such as purebred dogs, cats, and birds. The cage, toys, and supplies of high-quality cat or ferret food and other equipment averages about half of the purchase price of the animal. Of course, it is possible to buy a cage at almost any price one would choose.

A single adult ferret will consume as much as 5 to 8 pounds (2.5–4 kg) of high-quality dry cat food per month. Ferret food is usually slightly more expensive, but the ferret will tend to consume less because this food is more concentrated. Food consumption is higher in the fall and winter and lower in the spring and summer. Thus, food is not a major cost item for the maintenance of ferrets.

Ferrets can be easily groomed at home. It is not necessary to allow for the cost of grooming.

A yearly visit to the veterinarian is essential for distemper shots, rabies shots, if indicated, and a general health checkup. Costs vary widely for this service, so check in advance.

Housing and Equipment

Once you have decided that you wish to keep a ferret or several ferrets, you must prepare appropriate housing and obtain the equipment you will need to care for the animals and make them healthy and happy.

Housing

Your ferret's house can be a cage, an aquarium, or a small room in the house that has been "ferret-proofed." You can even let your ferret live outside year round, but if you want to do this, be sure to place the ferret outside for the first time during the summer. Then it will be able to adjust gradually to changes in temperature and cooler weather as winter approaches. If the ferret is left outside, it should have some shade—ferrets cannot tolerate high temperatures and should not be in direct sunlight. It will also need a small box or soft cloth to curl up in for sleeping. In the winter you must provide straw or other warm nesting material. There should be a roof over the whole cage to protect the ferret from wind and weather.

If you decide to house your ferret in a cage—and most people do—the cage should be at least 14 inches wide by 24 inches long and 10 inches high (about 35 × 60 × 24 cm). This size provides space for two adults to live

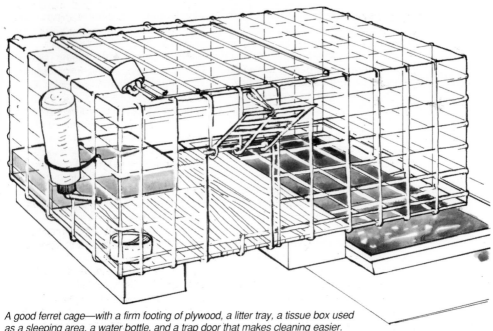

A good ferret cage—with a firm footing of plywood, a litter tray, a tissue box used as a sleeping area, a water bottle, and a trap door that makes cleaning easier.

Ferrets enjoy leaving their cages to socialize with their people.

comfortably if they also have some time out of the cage for play activities each day. Any cage design should provide a litter area, a feeding area, and a sleeping area. If you decide to use an open wire cage, a separate nest box for sleeping will have to be included.

Wire Cages

There are several types of cages that you can buy for your ferret, or you can try to make your own cage. Wire cages are the most popular. They come in two styles: trayed and trayless. A wire cage with a bottom tray may at first seem the better choice, but because ferrets use corners for latrines, much of the feces misses the tray and falls around the cage. A trayless cage is more suitable. It should be large enough to accommodate a litter box in one corner. The litter pan should have a low entry for the ferret and sides at least 4 inches (10 cm)

high to contain the feces. Many trayless cages have a wire floor that allows feces to fall through to a container or pad of paper below. This type of trayless cage with a wire floor is recommended because it makes cleaning much easier.

Wire cages are also the most popular of build-it-yourself type cages. Only a few tools are usually required to build most cages: pliers, a wire ringing tool, a hammer, and wire cutters.

A typical materials list to build a cage would be:
1 piece of 1 × 1 wire 4 feet × 24 inches (120 × 60 cm)
0.25 pound (0.1 kg) of small wire rings
8 penny box nails
1 piece of 0.25 inch (0.6 cm) aspenite 13 × 18 inches (33 cm × 46 cm)
2 wooden blocks about 2 × 4 × 12 inches (5 × 10 × 30 cm)
1 piece of 1 × 2 inch (2.5 × 5 cm) wire 10 × 14 inches (25 × 35 cm)

Ferrets can be kept outdoors, but they must be provided with some shade in warm weather.

The ferret's cage should have a separate litter box with one low edge to make it easy for the ferret to climb in and out.

The dimensions given here are the minimum; larger cages are fine if space permits in your home.

Other Types of Housing

Discarded aquariums are frequently used for ferrets because of their low cost and the excellent visibility they provide. Of course, they require a wire top to prevent the ferret from escaping. The major disadvantages of an aquarium as a ferret home is that there is little air movement at floor level, and cleaning the litter area becomes difficult.

Wooden boxes are also sometimes used to house ferrets, but this is not desirable. Wood retains moisture and germs, is difficult to clean, and impossible to sanitize. Wooden boxes also prevent the ferrets from seeing out, making them unable to observe and participate in their immediate surroundings.

The Litter Box and Litter

The ferret's litter box should have a low edge in the front and three high sides. The one low edge makes it easier for the ferret to climb in and out of the box. Since ferrets back all the way into a corner to urinate or defecate, you will want three high sides to prevent accidents over the edge. It is a good idea to leave some feces in the litter box until your ferret is com-

pletely trained. This helps to discourage the animal from playing in the litter. Any litter suitable for cats is fine for ferrets.

The Sleeping Area

The ferret needs a special nesting spot with appropriate bedding material for sleeping. The choice of nesting spot and bedding depends on the type of cage you are using. If you are using a wire cage, the ferret will be happier with a small box for a "hidey-hole." Your ferret will enjoy crawling in and out of the box and will not be happy with just a bare wire cage with no enclosed hiding spot. An upright tissue box or a plastic milk jug with holes cut out in several places make good ferret bedrooms. The nest house should be affixed to one end of the cage so it will not end up being moved to the litter end of the cage and becoming soiled.

If the cage and attached nesting box are to be kept outdoors, the bedding material can be hay, straw, wood chips, or other soft insulating material. You should avoid cedar chips, which have been known to cause respiratory problems in ferrets, and also sawdust, which can cause eye irritation.

If the cage and attached nesting box are to be kept indoors, the nest material can be soft cloth, cotton preferably. A soft cotton T-shirt or old towel makes a nice sleeping cover and can be washed easily.

If you are using an aquarium or other type of cage with closed bottom and sides, one section of it should be provided with bedding materials to serve as a sleeping corner. Any of the nesting materials mentioned above would be appropriate.

Food and Water Dishes

All ferrets need a constant supply of fresh food and water and you should purchase their food dishes and water bottles carefully.

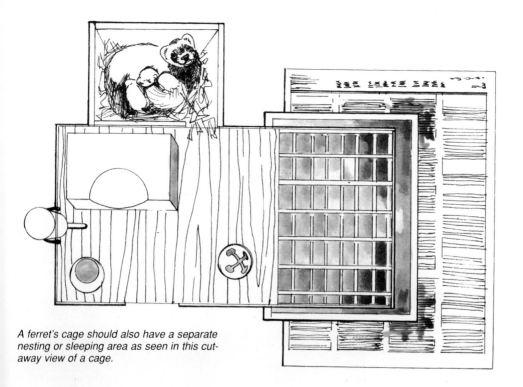

A ferret's cage should also have a separate nesting or sleeping area as seen in this cutaway view of a cage.

A heavy earthenware dish or shallow bowl is best for dry food. A lightweight dish is easily dumped and converted to a toy. Ferrets are strong for their body size and love to play with their dishes. If a lightweight dish is used, it must be attached to the cage so the ferret cannot move it.

If you are using a wire cage, a rabbit pellet hopper can be used for your ferret's food. Whether you decide to use an affixed food hopper or a heavy dish, be sure to place the food in the nesting area of the cage, not near the litter area where it can become soiled.

Water should also be supplied in the nesting area. Ferrets need a constant supply of fresh water. One easy way to supply this is to use rabbit water bottles that can be affixed to the side of the cage. Be sure, however, to attach the bottles low enough for the spout to be within easy reach of the ferret. With a new kit, touch its nose to the spout so that it knows where the water is.

All food and water dishes and bottles should be cleaned daily.

A heavy ceramic bowl is a good choice for ferrets.

19

Ferrets are enormously
curious creatures. They can
amuse themselves for hours simply
exploring their surroundings. Of
course this also means that you
must take care not to leave poten-
tially dangerous objects in their
play area.

Grooming Aids

You need certain items to keep your ferret well-groomed. It is best to purchase these items as soon as you bring your ferret home. In that way you will always be prepared to give it a bath and proper grooming.
The items you need are:
baby shampoo or shampoo approved for ferrets or cats—for bathing
regular bathroom towel—for drying
ordinary fingernail clippers—for trimming nails
ordinary nail file—for filing nails
stiff brush—to remove hair during twice-yearly coat changes

Ordinary nail clippers and cat claw scissors will both do an excellent job on your ferret's nails.

Collars and Leashes

It is wise to keep a collar on your ferret. If your pet should escape, the collar instantly alerts someone unfamiliar with ferrets—*this is a pet!* It is *not* some strange wild animal!

The ferret collar should be soft and lightweight. Nylon, suede, or soft leather is fine. If the collar is too bulky, the ferret will remove it. A small bell can be attached to the collar. This makes it easier to locate your pet in the house.

Ferrets can be trained to walk on leashes. Any lightweight leash suitable for a cat or small dog is fine. There are leashes available specifically for ferrets.

The main purpose of a collar is to help you locate your pet and to let others recognize the ferret as a PET should he or she go astray. Always use a collar with an elastic insert so the ferret can escape the collar if caught on something.

Toys

Any item that appeals to the ferret's sense of curiosity and adventure will be a treat for your pet. A good example of this is a clean plastic gallon jug with several 3-inch (7.5-cm) holes. The jug thus transformed becomes a playhouse, jungle trail, a secret hideout, and a perfect obstacle course for a game of chase.

Most cat toys, including balls, rubber squeak toys, furry creatures, and the like, will provide hours of fun for your pet. Check any rubber toys to be sure the ferret cannot pull off any part and swallow it. This could cause a life-threatening blocking. Catnip has no appeal for ferrets, but toys that contain it are acceptable.

Plastic pipe 3 inches (7.5 cm) in diameter with angles provides your ferret with

A large plastic jug with holes cut in it becomes a toy for ferrets who will climb in and out of it and hide in it.

A squeeze bottle is a handy way to dispense a treat—Linatone—to your ferret.

a safe place to explore. The more turns and corners in the pipe, the better.

Training Aids

There are several products that you can use to help you when you try to train your ferret. The vitamin-rich liquid Linatone is a treat for ferrets—they love it. It can be used as a reward for your ferret when it does what you wish, or it can be used to reinforce good experiences. Give a kit a drop or two when it is picked up and it will associate being picked up with a treat.

Linatone is an excellent coat supplement as well, helping to keep the fur smooth and furry. Be careful not to use too much, however. Linatone contains vitamin A and too much vitamin A accumulation is not beneficial for your pet. Therefore, limit its Linatone treats to 2 to 3 drops a day. A hair-coloring applicator bottle or similar type of squeeze bottle is a handy way to dispense the treat.

Just as ferrets like Linatone and will associate happy experiences with it, they dislike Bitter Apple. It can be used to train a ferret not to touch something. For example, ferrets sometimes become fascinated with curly telephone cords.

Bitter apple can be sprayed on the cord several times a day. After a few days, the ferret will lose all interest in chewing on the cord.

And, let's not forget perhaps the two best training aids—your voice and your hands.

Talk to your ferret. When it is good, speak in a soothing manner. If it is bad a sharp "no" or "stop" is quite effective. A ferret should be treated much like a new puppy.

Ferrets enjoy being stroked in the direction the hair lays. They prefer hard stroking rather than gentle patting. Never poke fingers at their noses.

If your ferret's play is too rough, a sound thump on the nose with your forefinger, accompanied by a sharp "no," will soon advise it that this is not acceptable behavior.

My tip: Never strike the ferret's body. This could cause an injury.

Ferrets like to be stroked firmly in the direction the hair lays.

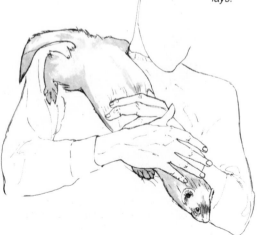

Adjusting to the New Home and General Care

Bringing Your Ferret Home

Before you bring your ferret home, you should learn as much as possible about ferrets. You should have your pet's bowls, food, and cage ready, and you should have some Linatone and Bitter Apple on hand.

Once you have determined where to buy your ferret, it is time to play with all the kits and adults available. Choose the one whose personality and color best suits you. Sometimes there is a kit who seems to choose you. We once had a young couple visit our farm who very definitely wanted a silver female. However, there was a sable male kit who flung himself into their hands every time they reached for their silver baby. They soon caved in to such delightful determination and home went the sable.

The trip home is generally enjoyable for the ferret as ferrets love to travel. You should bring a small cardboard box with papers in the bottom and some holes punched in the sides. Add some crumpled newspapers or paper towels for the ferret to crawl under

Ferrets are playful animals. They love to play with one another and to crawl in and out of boxes, trunks, and small spaces.

should it want to hide. As long as the animal seems calm, it is fine to hold it part of the way home. Should it get squirmy, place it in its box—it may be time for a bathroom visit.

Getting to Know Your Ferret

Now that you have your ferret home, it is time to get acquainted. If you have chosen a kit, remember, even though it is used to people, it is still a baby. The commotion of slamming doors and ringing phones, and the sensation of being alone may all be new experiences. A baby ferret will need its dry food soaked with water for several weeks and lots of attention. It does *not* need to go directly to a large party or every neighbor's house to be shown off. Give it a few weeks to get to know your family first. After that time, take it anywhere anytime.

An adult ferret will not need its food soaked with water and may require somewhat less attention, but remember, it too must get used to you, your family, and new surroundings.

When a kit wakes from its nap, allow it time to relieve itself and eat before a play or handling session. Speak in a soothing way and pick it up. Give it a drop of Linatone and walk around carrying it on your arm. A kit—and even an adult—will enjoy seeing the new sights with you. Stroke and tickle it just as you would a puppy. Carry it frequently as a kit, and it will pay off when it is an adult.

Allow the ferret to put its teeth gently on you in play. Mock combat is normal. The absolute rule is "If it hurts, the ferret is wrong and should be disciplined." Just like a new puppy, a young ferret must learn how rough to play.

Always curious, a ferret will play at an open cage door; it is always ready to get out and run around.

If you are going to allow your ferret free run, choose a small room and confine it there. It will need considerable time at first to explore its new surroundings before it is interested in playing. Once the ferret is thoroughly familiar with this area, it will be ready to interact with you. It will not need such a long exploration time after it has been in this area several times.

Basic Rules for Handling Ferrets

• Always speak in a soft, friendly manner to the ferret before picking it up—you do look *big* to it from down there.

• If the ferret is sleeping, allow it time to take care of litter trips and eating first.

• Give your ferret Linatone—not every time it is picked up—but often enough that it never knows when you'll do something wonderful for it.

• Do not be afraid to roughhouse with your ferret. It is small, but ferrets are used to playing roll and tumble games together; it does not want to be treated as though it were fragile.

• Do *not* put your pet down when it wants down. *You* must train *it*. Ferrets are smart enough to train you if you allow it. If it puts its teeth on you as a reminder (much like a cat gesture), give it a sharp *"no!"* If this is not sufficient, add a thump on the nose to the second *"no!"*

Playing with Your Ferret

Ferrets enjoy a variety of games. Hopping, jumping, and mock combat are normal for them. Ferrets also enjoy a good game of tug-of-war. Sometimes they will entice you to chase them and then they can chase you. Digging and burrowing—a pile of fall leaves is perfect—can elicit a hopping dance of joy on the part of your ferret. Any tube or container the ferret can crawl into and out of is fine. Hide and seek games seem to be a favorite.

Ouch! Baby Plays Too Rough

Ferrets have very tough skins. Both baby and adult ferrets play quite roughly with each other, but this is the cause of most problems that occur in ferret/human play. Since the ferret has

You must discipline your ferret. If a firm "No" is not enough, snap your fingers.

learned the level of pressure it may exert on its brothers and sisters without making them angry, it is logical for it to expect you to enjoy the same vigorous games. If you are consistent in your discipline and correct your ferret each time it is too rough, it soon learns that its new two-footed friend requires it to be more careful. If you only correct the ferret sometimes and not others, you are making it very difficult for it to understand what you expect.

Nipping Toes

Toe nipping is the most common misbehavior of young ferrets. It seems to happen for two reasons: not making the connection between the wiggling creatures and their two-legged friend, and a desire to play chase and have interaction.

Either reason requires the same response: *firm discipline*. A sharp *"no!"* spoken about 6 inches (15 cm) from the ferret's face while making eye contact is most effective. If you have a toe nipper, spray Bitter Apple on your socks and then tempt the ferret. It quickly learns that the enticing, wiggling creatures inside the sock taste *terrible* and loses all desire to grab them.

My tip: The real danger is that you might make the mistake of inadvertantly encouraging your ferret to form the toe-biting habit. If you are amused by the first gentle nibbles and allow the behavior to continue, you reinforce a pattern that inevitably will become intolerable for you.

Toe biting must never be allowed to start as a cute game. Stop it before it gets to be a habit.

One good way to carry a ferret: the ferret's underside is held in one hand, its lower back in the other.

You may also want to carry your ferret this way, supporting its chest area with one hand, its tail end with the other.

Give your ferret Linatone often enough so it never knows just when you are going to do something wonderful for it. Here, the author is giving her friend a much-appreciated treat.

Baskets, boxes, and empty cardboard tubes all make fine playthings for your new pet.

HOW-TO:
Grooming and Bathing

The correct way to trim a ferret's nails.

In recent years ferrets have become so popular that many professional groomers and pet salons are accustomed to doing them. However, ferrets are relatively easy to groom, and you may wish to groom your ferrets yourself. If so, follow these simple guidelines.

Ears and nails

The hardest part of grooming a ferret is the care of the ears and the nails. When you are cleaning the ears, it is best if the ferret is held by a helper. The helper should use one hand to grasp the ferret around the shoulders, forelegs, and chest in a firm, but gentle, manner. The helper should hold a bottle of Linatone in his or her other hand and use the Linatone to distract the ferret while the ear cleaning procedure goes on.

The tiny ears of a ferret are cleaned with cotton tips and peroxide. Dip the tip of the cotton tip into the peroxide and squeeze off any excess. Then carefully place the cotton tip into the outer ear area and gently wipe out any debris and excess wax.

Cutting the nails is another important grooming task. The nails of a ferret should be cut just short of the vein. Look at a ferret's nails and you will see the red vein running down inside the nail. A cat-type nail cutter is the proper size nail clipper to use on your ferret.

However, you can also use a regular nail clipper used for humans, but remember to turn the clipper sideways so it won't snip the toe when you trim the nails.

After doing the ears and the nails, you have completed the hardest grooming tasks and are ready to comb out any loose hairs on your ferret. Use a soft nylon brush to comb out the loose hairs. Brushing also stimulates the skin of the ferret.

Bathing

Now, you are ready to bathe your ferret. A double sink works best. Fill both sinks with lukewarm water. Wet and shampoo the ferret in one sink using tearless ferret or cat shampoo or a tearless baby shampoo. Then rinse the ferret. Use the second sink for final rinsing to be sure that all shampoo is removed.

After the bathing is finished, you may want to use a cat-approved flea dip or a lanolin-based cream rinse. Do not use dog products for your ferret.

They are often too strong and could be dangerous. When finished, rub the ferret vigorously with a bath towel to help it dry and then keep it in a warm, draft-free room until it is completely dry.

Coat Changes

Ferrets change coats completely twice a year. In the young, the kit coat gives way to the first adult coat. This is a short, lightweight coat. The second coat is a long, dense beautiful winter coat. At the time that a ferret changes into a winter coat, it puts on quite a bit of weight. After the winter months, it will reduce its food consumption, drop weight, and return to its lightweight coat. In the house, it is tidier to brush the ferret often during the period when it is losing its winter coat. Most of what would be shed out around the house will brush out easily and can be discarded.

Wet the ferret thoroughly before applying soap.

Be sure to rinse the ferret thoroughly so that no traces of soap remain.

Using a ferret or cat shampoo, wash your ferret carefully.

Towel dry the ferret after its bath and then let it stay in a warm place for a while.

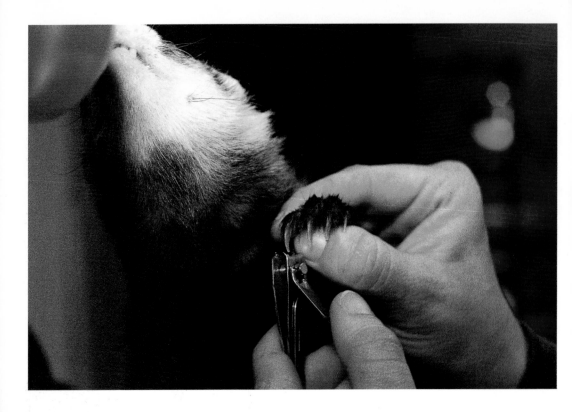

Nail trimming should be a part of regular care.

Ferrets and Other Animals

Ferret play with other animals (cross-species interaction) is one of the most intriguing aspects of ferret behavior. We have heard stories from all across the country about ferret play with cats, parakeets, dogs, rabbits, small rodents, and other animals. However, care must be taken in the first few meetings between ferrets and their new friends.

Some do's and don'ts:

• **Do** restrain each animal until it is aware of the other animal or animals. Surprises can lead to tragedy.

• **Do** be prepared to separate the animals at the first sign of trouble.

• **Do** be *especially* careful when introducing rodents. Ferrets can be predators of these animals.

• **Don't** rush the friendship. Cats especially like to approach new relationships over a longer time period.

• **Don't** neglect other pets or make them jealous. This leads to aggressive behavior.

• **Don't** leave mixed groups together unsupervised until you are certain few problems will occur.

• **Don't** worry about mixing ferrets together except unneutered males. All others will get along fine. They will play very rough and will establish who is boss but almost never injure each other.

• **Don't** mix dogs who have been trained to hunt small animals with ferrets. Some of these dogs adapt well to ferrets but others are quick to kill.

If the initial meeting is carefully supervised...

a dog and a ferret can learn to play together peacefully.

Two old friends going for a stroll with their person...

pause to enjoy a quiet moment in the shade.

HOW-TO:
Training Your Ferret

You must train your ferret—for the ferret's happiness and long life as well as for your own full enjoyment of it. For reasons of safety and hygiene, it must be trained to the cage and litter box. To increase your enjoyment and the ferret's, you may also train your ferret to the leash, to the shoulder or hood, and to sit up.

To the Cage

Ferrets, unlike cats, do not mind small places. Given a choice, ferrets will curl up in a small ball in a quiet, hidden cubbyhole. This lack of fear makes them very comfortable in a cage. They need and want to be out of the cage for fun, play, and exploring, but—come nap time—they are content to return to the cage.

Ferrets are much safer in a cage than loose in an empty house. The best job of "ferret proofing" the house still leaves open the possibility of danger from unexpected guests who may unintentionally injure your pet by stepping on a throw rug which has become a ferret cover.

To the Litter Box

Ferrets are latrine-type animals and prefer to relieve themselves in the same place every time. This instinct makes them easy to housebreak.

Housebreaking in an open area should start in a small room (a half bath is ideal). Place the litter box with some feces in it in a corner. The ferret will use it easily. Expand the space available to it gradually and it will return to the box.

In a large house, two litter pans may be necessary. With such short legs, the ferret will appreciate not having to go too far to its box and will have few accidents.

In a cage containing a litter box, be sure the litter box entrance is flat with sides at least 3 inches (7.5 cm) high. Place some manure in one corner and the ferret will soon use it as a bathroom.

Most ferrets relieve themselves within several minutes of awakening. This habit allows you to see to it that the proper facility is used. One friend of ours rewarded her ferret so often for good hygiene habits that the ferret learned to pretend to go and would then run over for Linatone rewards.

Should your ferret choose the wrong place in which to relieve itself, use a sharp *"no!"* and a loud clap of the hands. Quickly place the ferret in the proper

Your ferret will be very happy within the safety of its cage.

area and insist it stay there until it attends to business. Reward your ferret with Linatone or other treats for being good.

To the Shoulder or Hood

Training to the shoulder or the hood of a jacket is the easiest way to carry your ferret on visits to new places. Stand or kneel over a trash can filled with crumpled newspaper. Place the kit on your shoulder or in the hood and allow it to crawl around until it stops paying attention to its balance.

Most litter pans need a cut down section so the ferret can easily enter the box.

When it starts to fall, say *"no!"* in a loud tone and allow it to fall in the newspapers. The loud *no,* coupled with falling and the loud rustling of the papers, induces enough fear to make it more careful. Do this several times and then stop for that session. It usually takes five or six sessions to train the ferret, but from then on it will stay and be careful of its balance.

After your ferret is completely trained, put it down if it becomes excited or very active while on the shoulder or hood. It may have to go to the litter box.

To the Leash

We have never known of a ferret that is leash trained like a dog is. Leash training in ferrets means keeping them from constantly fighting the leash—they will not learn to heel.

Use a lightweight leash attached to your ferret's collar (no choke chains, please) and allow it to drag the leash around the house to get used to it. After this period, start restraining your pet

For outside trips, it is best to keep your ferret in a harness.

while sitting in a chair in a familiar room. Being used to the area will make it easier to restrain the ferret at first. Once it learns the futility of fighting the leash, you are ready for a trip outside.

Start in the yard and allow it to move in a circle with you as the center point. After several 10-minute sessions over a period of several days, you should start to encourage it to follow in the direction you wish to travel. Much patience is needed, but it will learn! From now on practice is all that is needed.

To Sit Up

The sit-up is the easiest of all tricks to teach ferrets; it can be accomplished in a few 5-minute sessions.

Start by putting Linatone on your finger and letting your ferret lick it. Gradually raise your finger higher and it will naturally follow it. Keep plenty of Linatone on your finger. As your ferret begins to sit up praise it generously. If it reaches out to hold your finger take it away

Most ferrets can be trained to stay on your shoulder.

and start over. If you repeat the command *"sit"* in a gentle voice as this is done, the ferret will soon understand the connection. Be sure to reward it often at first. Later it will not be necessary to give it a reward every time. Any word can be used as a command, but the same word must be used all the time.

Running Around the House

Ferrets enjoy exploring in the house. Once they have investigated everything they will be ready to play. The typical ferret will explore by traveling around the edges of the room and visiting the underside of every piece of furniture. It is futile to attempt to interest it in games in a new area until it is satisfied it has seen everything in the area.

Ferrets love to go places with you and can be trained to sit on your shoulder.

Taking Your Ferret in the Car

All the ferret owners we know love to take their pets visiting. Ferrets love car trips, and we have never seen a carsick ferret.

Before taking your ferret on a trip, check your car carefully to see that there are no "ferret doors." Check the firewall under the dash, under the seats, and behind the rear seat for holes leading out of the car. Many people let their ferret have the run of the car. Some paper with a smear of feces placed in one corner of the car will tell it where the bathroom is. This has always worked well for us when we travel with our pet ferrets. Some people prefer to carry a small litter pan that the ferret has been accustomed to using. A small portable cage with a bed and a litter pan is handy for ferret car travel.

Never leave a ferret in the car in the summer with the windows closed.

They are quite sensitive to the heat. Imagine yourself there while wearing a fur coat.

If the ferret is traveling in a carrier or cage, don't let it sit in the sun for any length of time.

With these simple rules you will love traveling with your pets as much as we do.

Taking Your Ferret on Vacation

Because ferrets love to travel and are so confident and curious, they are very little trouble on vacation.

You must take a portable cage with you for your convenience and your pet's safety. Use this cage to contain it at the motels or homes where you are staying. It is not possible to check each location for hidden dangers, so supervise play time carefully.

A supply of dry ferret or cat food and clean water must be offered frequently.

They can also be trained to sit in the hood of a jacket.

Because water bottles leak and cups or bowls spill, offer these at each stop.

For airline travel, an underseat cat carrier is available. This will enable you to "carry on" your pet. Be sure you declare your pet when making flight reservations, as sometimes there are limits to the number of pets allowed on the plane.

Almost all motels will allow caged ferrets if you speak with them ahead of time. Advance notification will prevent maids and service people from becoming frightened if they don't know what a ferret looks like.

Traveling to Foreign Countries

The basic rules for international travel are simple. First, check with the embassy of the country you are going to visit for their rules concerning ferrets. Also, be sure to register your pet with U.S. Customs before leaving.

In our travels to Mexico and Canada, we have never encountered problems. The registration with U.S. Customs allowed us to bring our pets back into the United States without a quarantine period. However, laws are always subject to change and it is important to check each trip before putting your pet at risk.

It is best to bottle water and carry your own cat food from home in order to avoid stress for your pet.

Leaving Your Ferret

For One Day

In almost all homes a one- or two-day absence—without a sitter—causes no problems. Be sure to leave an ample supply of food and water in the ferret's cage. Make absolutely sure the ferret cannot accidentally spill its

A well-ventilated basket can be used when you travel with your ferret in the car.

food and water—leaving itself hungry and thirsty during your absence. Research has shown the ferret to have a "three-hour digestive system." This means that what the ferret eats is through its system and gone in three hours. Therefore, the ferret needs a constant supply of food or it becomes *very* hungry in a short period of time. Turn on a radio or television to provide some company. For a two-day

Many airlines require an animal carrier like this for a ferret.

absence, have a neighbor peek in at least once to be sure all is well.

If your ferret normally has the "run of the house," accustom it to its cage while you are home. It is not fair to change its whole routine at the same time it must be alone.

For a Short Vacation

In circumstances where your ferret cannot travel with you on vacation, you should leave it with a good "ferret sitter." The sitter should have the following information and supplies:
• A schedule of your ferret's normal activity times.
• Plenty of food.
• Complete instructions for how to operate cages, bowls, feeders, water bottles, and other equipment.
• A phone number where you can be reached.
• The name and phone number of your veterinarian in case of injury or illness.
• The names and numbers of any other ferret owners who may be able to help in an emergency.

An owner of a ferret is the first choice for a "sitter," but anyone who is responsible about animal welfare can do the job. It is best to leave the ferret with the sitter on a trial basis for a day or so before leaving on a trip. This practice run will point out any problems and give you time to work out solutions before the actual trip.

For Longer Periods

For extended periods away from home, it is important that the ferret sitter has a more thorough knowledge of ferrets. Changes in weight, diet, bowel habits, and signs of illness must be understood by the sitter.

As a general rule, it is better to leave your pet in a cat kennel. Ferret care is closer to cat care than to dog care. Of course, the care varies with the personnel, knowledge, and facilities of each kennel. The attitude of the personnel is very important. We would never leave our animals at a kennel where the staff was afraid or leery of ferrets. When there is a close decision between the facilities and knowledge, we prefer a staff with a real liking for ferrets.

When friends or family are caring for your pets, it is a good idea to have a back-up sitter in case an emergency develops at the first home.

Neutering Your Ferret

Neutering is part of good care for your ferret. It is necessary to save the health—and life—of a female and to reduce the odor and aggressiveness of a male. The majority of ferrets sold today have already been neutered and de-scented. If you are unable to obtain a ferret that has already been altered, you will need to make arrangements with your veterinarian to have this done as soon as possible.

Female

All female ferrets must be spayed sooner or later to protect their lives. Aplastic anemia and septicemia—two diseases that are a direct result of prolonged heat in females—are the leading causes of death in female ferrets.

Approximately two weeks after the beginning of the heat season, high levels of estrogen cause the vulva to swell greatly. The vulva becomes enormous. If left unspayed, the vulva will stay swollen and become damp and open. This leads to the life-threatening health risks for your female. The moist enlarged opening is a natural channel for infection—which frequently leads to septicemia and death. At the same time, the prolonged high estrogen level leads to aplastic anemia.

The only way to stop the prolonged heat—and the nearly always fatal diseases associated with it—is to breed an unspayed female. But breeding a female every time she comes into heat is a great drain on her body, and it too leads to severe health problems.

For these reasons, it becomes absolutely necessary to spay females at some point in their lives. Spaying can be done at any age. Most veterinarians prefer that it be done before 6 to 8 months of age, but certainly before she is in heat. Estrus causes an increase in blood supply and enlargement of the ovaries and reproductive tract that makes surgery more risky. If your ferret should come into heat before she is spayed, your veterinarian *cannot* wait to spay the ferret until she cycles naturally out of estrus. This may take months, and she could easily die of aplastic anemia—even on the first heat.

Male

Castration of male ferrets is a simple, almost risk-free operation. It can be performed at any age, but six to eight weeks is the ideal time. Older males require up to several months for the benefits of neutering to fully appear. The only reason we can see *not* to neuter males is to keep them for breeding purposes. Neutering causes a dramatic decrease in odor. Unneutered males must be bathed daily to make them acceptable as house pets.

Neutering lowers aggression. During breeding season an intact male may injure or kill other ferrets; both males and females may be included in their victims. However, no aggression is directed toward people.

Neutered ferrets are no more likely to become sluggish, lazy, and fat than unaltered animals. Ferrets gain weight at the same time they grow their heavy winter coats. They lose weight and become thinner and more active when they grow their lighter summer fur coats. These natural changes can happen at any time of the year when ferrets are kept indoors year-round.

This beautifully groomed sable ferret makes it easy to understand the popularity of raccoon-like markings.

The white-footed butterscotch is still relatively rare. This ferret has four white feet.

HOW-TO:
Avoiding Hazards

Ferret Proofing Your Home—Hidden Home Dangers

Because ferrets are so small and love dark, tight places, there are special safety considerations for ferrets. Here is a list of problem areas.

Refrigerator motors: Make sure your ferret cannot get under the refrigerator. They love the area close to the fan and can easily be injured.

Chair or sofa springs: Make sure the ferret has not crawled into the springs to nap before you sit down.

Chair cushions: Make sure the ferret is not sleeping under the cushion before you sit down.

Lumpy throw rugs: Beware! That lump could be your dozing pet.

Buckets of Lysol and other cleaners: Ferrets have been known to go to great trouble to drink this poison. Never leave your ferret outside its cage while you have cleaning supplies in use.

If the ferret can fit its head through an opening, the flexible body will follow.

Always check for ferrets before you sit down.

Small opening to the outdoors: An adult ferret can squeeze through anything larger than 1 × 2 inches (2.5 × 5 cm). Check carefully for openings before uncaging your ferret.

Refrigerator doors: Make sure the ferret does not decide to investigate the refrigerator or freezer while the door is open. Unnoticed it can be accidentally shut in. Check for your ferret before closing doors.

Washer and dryer vents are a means of escape for many ferrets. Make sure all hoses are securely attached.

Recliner chairs are one of the leading causes of injuries to ferrets. Never move the recliner without first locating your ferret.

If Your Ferret Escapes

We frequently get calls saying "My ferret is lost. What should I do?" Beyond the obvious, "Look around the house carefully, it may just be asleep in some hidden corner," there are some other things to do:

Make a list of 10 places in the home the ferret can't possibly be. Then look there. This list worked for one of our callers who found a cold and hungry pet caught in the freezer side of her side-by-side refrigerator.

Organize a search of the yard and surrounding houses. Concentrate on holes, foundations, old buildings, wood piles, and any other places that may lure your lost pet.

Alert neighbors that your pet is gone.

Put up notices at stores, laundry centers, and other public places.

Alert your mail person and other delivery people.

Offer a reward.

At this time you certainly will be happy that your ferret has a collar and bell so it will not be mistaken for a wild animal and killed out of fear!

Common Accidents

Indoors and out there are several types of accidents that commonly cause injuries to ferrets. Below is a list of common ones and basic first aid.

Indoors

Burns: Apply ice to the affected area and take your pet to the veterinarian if serious burns occur. For minor burns, vitamin E cream seems to be effective in promoting skin healing.

Crushing: This accident comes from being stepped on or caught in doors, springs, chair cushions, etc. The main risk here is internal injury. Your veterinarian should examine the pet if there is any doubt.

Back injury: This also occurs from being stepped on or from

Watch for ferrets when walking. Be especially careful of any "lumps" under throw rugs.

accidental falls. Watch closely for signs of slow or painful movement, paralysis, or dragging a leg. Take the ferret to your veterinarian at once for this kind of injury.

Poison: In the event of accidental poisoning, speed is of the essence. Get medical help at once. It is important to take the container of poison

Never leave your ferret alone outside. Ferrets are fearless and will approach animals that will harm them.

with you if you can be sure of the cause.

Outdoors

Caught in car door: This type of accident usually results in internal injuries because of the weight and speed of the door. Always consult your veterinarian.

Fight with other animals: Usually ferrets can defend themselves quite well. They seem to know no fear. They will fight almost anything if the opponent starts it. General first aid should be used for minor injuries. For serious cuts, tears, and broken limbs, consult your veterinarian immediately.

Accidental escapes: After being lost for several days, ferrets are usually dehydrated and malnourished. Medical attention is usually needed. A checkup at this time is money well spent.

This ferret enjoys a little nourishment while out for a stroll with its person.

Proper Nutrition

Ferrets basically regulate their own food consumption. Food passes through the ferret's digestive tract in only three hours so a constant supply of food and water is necessary. The diet should consist mainly of dry ferret food or a top quality premium dry cat food.

The biggest variable in most animal foods is the quality of the protein. Ferrets do best with a high percentage of animal protein. Unfortunately, however, most pet foods are labeled with the total percentage of protein but not with the percentage of vegetable protein or animal protein. Some protein-rich foods contain soy products and other cereals that raise the total protein percentage to an acceptable level of 30 percent, but much of this is vegetable protein. With food containing high-cereal protein, the ferret is forced to consume large amounts of food in order to meet its nutritional needs. On the other hand, with foods rich in animal protein the ferret consumes less and is better nourished. Less consumption is better for the ferret and makes cleaning litter boxes easier for you. When purchasing food for your ferret, be sure to read the list of ingredients. Choose feed with animal protein listed as the first or second ingredient. This means there is a higher percent of animal base protein in the feed. Animal protein is more easily digested than vegetable proteins.

What Type of Food

We recommend feed formulated specifically for ferrets. If you are unable to obtain ferret food, purchase a *premium* dry cat food such as Science Diet, Iams, or Eukanuba in your pet store. The results show in the health of the ferret. Many major brands of cat food sold in grocery stores and supermarkets are probably satisfactory too, but beware of low cost brands that may achieve the low cost by the use of large amounts of vegetable protein.

Food is available in both dry and moist forms. Dry food has many advantages:
• it stays fresh longer and does not spoil or sour as quickly as canned food.
• it usually contains lower ash sodium, and other minerals that may be harmful to ferrets than does wet food.
• it contains little or no milk, which is not healthy for ferrets.
• the dry pellets help keep the ferret's teeth and gums in good condition.
• dry foods cost less.
• the storage and feeding of dry foods are easier.

The only drawback to dry food for ferrets is that no moisture is provided and you must remember to supply plenty of fresh water to aid the ferret in digesting its food. Canned foods contain lots of water in the food mixture.

There has been little long-term experience with the use of packaged moist foods for ferrets.

What Ferrets Drink

Water is the liquid of choice for ferrets, although some ferrets will drink small amounts of fruit juice. Cow's milk should not be given to ferrets as it generally leads to diarrhea. Goat's milk can be given to

There are several good feeds that are formulated specifically for ferrets. Ask your pet store to order some for you. Moist cat food is not recommended.

small kits to supplement mother's milk with no ill effects.

The Food and Weight Gain Cycle

The amount of food required and the weight gain of ferrets normally vary with the seasons. Under natural lighting conditions ferrets eat a lot and gain large amounts of weight in the fall. This prepares them for the cold winter months. The extra food is stored as fat providing insulation for the animal during the cold winter months. In the spring, as the amount of light increases, ferrets tend to lose most of their body fat. This prepares them for summer heat—even with a fur coat.

Ferrets kept inside all year-round in light-filled houses, and at night near a night light, take time to adjust and their seasonal changes do not correspond to the calendar. If there is no medical problem, weight losses and gains can usually be explained by the unnatural lighting conditions under which the ferret lives.

Special Nutrition Needs

There are several times in a ferret's life cycle when its nutritional needs are special: when it is very young, when it is pregnant, and when it is very old.

In the Young Animal

Kits from weaning (6 weeks) to about 14 weeks of age require special care. Water can be added to their dry ration until it is even with the top of the food. After standing for 10 to 15 minutes, the food becomes soft and more attractive to the kit. A few drops of Linatone or a tiny amount of kitten milk replacer added to the mixture often stimulates the kits' appetites.

Ferrets achieve 90 percent of their adult size in the first 14 weeks, so food consumption is very high. In fact,

A cage-mounted water bottle.
Caution: It takes some ferrets longer to learn to use this type water system. Keep a water bowl available until you are sure your ferret can use a bottle.

a kit of about 8 to 12 weeks old will eat as much as an adult female.

In the young kit, we restrict treats to once or twice weekly in order to be sure all the nutritional building blocks are in place for the rapid growth. We certainly don't want any kit to wait for treats and neglect its normal food.

For slow-growing kits, goat's milk added to the soft food provides additional protein in a readily available form. Milk replacers designed for kittens are also useful.

For undernourished kits who must be weaned somewhat early, small amounts of Nutri-cal or other supplement give a high dose of calories in a small quantity. The baby should also be eating softened hard food to ensure proper nutrition. Milk replacers should be mixed in as well.

In the Old Animal
When ferrets reach seven or eight years of age, a few special needs must be met. Adding ½ teaspoon of vegetable oil to the food once every day or so helps the ferrets maintain a better coat and seems to aid in digestion and bowel movement.

Be sure to watch older animals closely for any signs of difficulty in chewing. This can indicate teeth problems. You may need to start adding water to soften the dry food for ease of chewing and take the animal to the veterinarian.

A high-quality ferret food or petstore-type cat food is especially important for older ferrets. With advancing age animals do not absorb the nutritional levels they need as readily.

In the Pregnant Animal
It is imperative that the breeding animal be of good weight—if she is too fat there can be birthing difficulties; if she is too thin the stress of breeding and raising young can threaten her life. Try to give the highest quality food at this time.

Be sure your pet is receiving a high-quality feed. Many people also add a small amount of boiled liver two to three times weekly during the last weeks of pregnancy and during the kit-raising period. A small amount of milk replacer can also be used. It is important not to feed high amounts of supplemental meat without adding calcium. Higher levels of phosphorus than calcium can lead to severe health problems in all mammals.

Nutrition Disorders
While it is difficult to prove that any particular illness is due to poor nutrition, it is certain that the nutritionally deprived ferret is more susceptible to nearly all diseases. Ferrets are susceptible to an unknown enteritis (inflammation of the intestinal tract) that can appear during times of stress (coat changes, breeding, etc.) or when the ferret is run-down. Poor nutrition increases the possibility of this condition. Unknown enteritis must be treated swiftly or the ferret will die.

Treats
Almost anything the ferret enjoys—no bones please—can be used for treats. The important thing to remember is that they are just that—*treats*. Giving treats should not be confused with providing a nutritionally balanced diet. In limited quantities, treats will not harm your pet.

Almost all ferrets enjoy Linatone and a few drops daily are beneficial. We once had a ferret who loved red licorice and came running at the rattle of the bag. We know of another ferret who loved lima beans—soft centers only—all skins were spit out under the counter. Frequently ferrets are not adventuresome eaters; you may have to introduce something several times before your ferret will try anything new.

If you notice changes in your ferret's behavior or appearance, you must act quickly to remedy the situation.

When Your Ferret Is Sick

A high-quality ferret food or premium dry cat food, a few drops of Linatone daily, plenty of fresh water, a yearly vaccination program for canine distemper, and an observant owner will keep most ferrets safe and healthy. Ferrets are so small that you do not have time to wait and observe a problem for several days. If you notice changes in your ferret's appearance or behavior, you must act quickly to try to correct the problem. The following section may well save your pet's life—read it carefully.

The Home Health Check
• **Check** for clear bright eyes and an alert expression. Watering eyes or a dull and listless expression are frequently the first signs of general health problems.
• **Check** the whiskers. Are they long and soft? Short, broken whiskers usually indicate a poor diet. Hair is almost pure protein and its appearance is a good indicator of protein intake.
• **Check** by rubbing your hands gently all over the ferret to try to detect lumps of any kind. A lump may be a tumor, which should be removed, or it may be an abscess resulting from an infection. Abscesses most often occur in the area of the jaw.
• **Check** the ferret's coat and skin carefully. Look for even growth of the coat and be sure that there are no fleas or ticks. A brush used over a white piece of paper will dislodge debris and dirt from the coat. Examine the brushed-out particles and if any move, you will know that the ferret has fleas.
• **Check** the anal area closely for signs of diarrhea, bleeding, or infection.
• **Check** for any signs of discharge from the vulva in females, and from the opening of the penal sheath in males. A discharge is usually a sign of infection and calls for a visit to the veterinarian.
• **Check** the ferret's weight. The ferret should not be too fat or too thin but in proportion to its overall size. The ideal is a slender, athletic-looking animal.
• **Check** the ears for signs of a black waxlike substance; this could indicate ear mites or other problems.
• **Check** your pet's stools on a regular basis. If it has black tarry stools, upper intestinal bleeding is occurring. If your ferret has not had a stool for several days, it may have an internal blockage. Either situation is critical and requires a trip to the veterinarian.

Common Diseases and Disorders
Ferrets, like other animals, are subject to various infectious diseases, intestinal disorders, parasitic infestations, and physical injuries. In addition, they are also subject to blocked scent glands and females to aplastic anemia and septicemia.

Common Infectious Diseases
Ferrets are susceptible to many infectious diseases, chief among

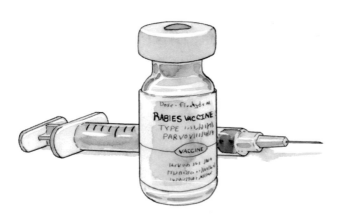

Be sure you visit your veterinarian at least once a year to keep your pet current on necessary vaccinations.

per. Ferrets are highly susceptible to it, and it is fatal. If you wait until the animal already has canine distemper, it will probably die. Vaccination is imperative. The kit must be at least 12 weeks of age to be sure the adult shot will give immunity. Kits may be given "baby shots" before 12 weeks of age, but they must still receive a shot at 12 weeks or older to be protected properly. After that, vaccinate yearly to be sure protection is provided.

Warning: Vaccine should be modified-live. It should *not* be of ferret tissue origin. Ferret tissue origin vaccine injected into a ferret *will give the ferret distemper*.

Rabies: According to the United States Center for Disease Control in Atlanta, Georgia, there have been very few documented cases of rabies in ferrets. Although ferrets are certainly susceptible to rabies if bitten by a rabid animal, ferrets are usually kept indoors and simply are not in circumstances where exposure to rabies is likely. However, there is always the risk of the ferret escaping and coming in contact with a rabid animal.

Fortunately, there is now a rabies vaccine available for your ferret. These vaccines are approved specifically for use in ferrets. Your veterinarian will be able to recommend a rabies vaccination schedule for your pet. One big plus for vaccination is that if your ferret should scratch or nip a person or another animal, you can advise those involved that your pet is vaccinated. Otherwise, they may want to destroy your pet to check the ferret for rabies. This could be a needless tragedy.

Aplastic Anemia and Septicemia in Females

Aplastic anemia and septicemia are the leading causes of death in female ferrets. If a female is not spayed or repeatedly bred there is about a 90 percent chance that she will die in the

them colds, flu, pneumonia, and canine distemper.

Colds and Flu: Ferrets catch the same type of colds and flu that people catch. Like any new family member, a ferret can catch a cold from you and give it back to you. The ferret usually has the good sense to drink plenty of liquids and get plenty of rest until it has recovered—usually in three to seven days.

Pneumonia: The symptoms of pneumonia in ferrets are the same as in a person—namely, labored or rattly breathing, a fever, and signs of a cold persisting beyond the normal few days. The ferret must be taken to the veterinarian for an antibiotic to help it recover.

Feline Distemper: There is conflicting information about feline distemper. Many experts claim that ferrets are not susceptible to it. Nevertheless, there have been several reports of cases of feline distemper in ferrets. None of these cases has been confirmed with diagnostic testing. It is, however, safe to assume that it is not a common occurrence. An inexpensive feline distemper vaccination could prove to be worthwhile insurance for your ferret. Check with your veterinarian for his recommendation.

Canine Distemper: There is no confusion concerning canine distem-

first heat season. It is best to purchase a pet that is already spayed and de-scented to avoid this risk. If your ferret is not already altered, contact your veterinarian immediately. (See page 39.)

Intestinal Disorders

Changes in the consistency and frequency of bowel movements can signal disease in your ferret—serious illness or a reaction to a change in diet or a period of stress.

Diarrhea: If your ferret has a very soft stool or diarrhea, first eliminate all treats. The usual cause of diarrhea is food that contains a high percentage of milk, such as ice cream or cottage cheese. A sudden change in feed can also cause a day or two of soft stools.

Your ferret can also have intestinal flu. This is usually associated with greenish loose stool for a day or two, after which the ferret is back to normal.

With continued diarrhea, dehydration is the biggest risk, with the ferret not taking in as much liquid as it is losing. This can be life threatening. You should then take your ferret to the veterinarian, who can inject fluid under the skin in several places. The ferret absorbs this fluid gradually and this greatly reduces the risk of dehydration while the cause of the diarrhea is being corrected.

Black Tarry Stools: Black tarry stools indicate gastrointestinal bleeding and are frequently associated with enteritis, an inflammation of the intestinal tract, and with times of stress, such as coat changes and heat. A "wait and see how it is tomorrow" attitude can easily cost your pet its life. The symptoms cannot be ignored. Consult your veterinarian. Be sure to follow your veterinarian's advice on what dosage and how many days to administer any medication. And, be sure that your ferret drinks plenty of water while being treated. Some drugs

can be hard on the kidneys and ferrets are somewhat susceptible to kidney problems. Drinking water seems to reduce the risk of developing kidney complications.

Note: The first stool after whelping is black-tarry, but this is normal.

Lack of Stool: The absence of any stool for a 24-hour period should not be taken lightly. The most frequent cause of this is an internal blockage. This may result from the ferret's swallowing of a small piece of foam rubber or other small object. Lack of stool, especially if accompanied by vomiting, must be dealt with promptly. Ferrets are simply too small to have enough body reserves to postpone treatment. It is frequently necessary to x-ray the ferret to locate the blockage and then to go in surgically to remove it. The survival chances of the ferret are substantially higher if the operation is performed before the animal becomes weak.

Note: Any animal who is sick and not eating much will have little stool, but this does not indicate a blockage. It is better to check with your veterinarian early on concerning any potential problems.

Vomiting: Ferrets seldom vomit. If, however, the ferret has an intestinal virus, it may sometimes vomit. This is often accompanied by soft, greenish stool. The symptoms usually disappear in a few days.

On the other hand, if the ferret is vomiting and has had no stool for 24 hours, take it to the veterinarian immediately. It is very likely that the animal has a blockage and may well need surgery. Do not wait to see how it is doing tomorrow.

Occasionally ferrets will make a gagging sound as if to vomit but will only bring up a small amount of liquid. This happens most frequently at coat change time and is probably caused by hair in the throat.

lem, the ferret will have to be de-scented, or, in other words, have the scent glands surgically removed. Many people prefer to purchase a kit that is already de-scented and avoid the problem completely.

Parasitic Infestations

Ferrets are not commonly bothered by any parasitic infestations. The only exception is heartworm, and heart-worm infestation has been found in only a small percentage of ferrets.

Heartworm in ferrets can be traced to an epidemic of heartworms in dogs on the coast of Maryland in the 1950s when a small number of fer-rets were also infested. However, to the author's knowledge, no other sig-nificant heartworm outbreaks have been reported.

Research indicates that while ferrets may become infested with heart-worms, they do not transmit them.

The common worms of dogs and cats are not generally found in fer-rets. Therefore there is no need for regular deworming of your pet. Yearly stool checks by your veteri-narian are recommended.

Eye Problems

Ferrets sometimes become blind in or have cataracts on one or both eyes. If you suspect that your ferret is hav-ing vision problems, take it to the vet-erinarian to determine if anything can be done. Blind ferrets do not seem to have difficulty in getting around or playing. They use their other senses and appear to lead a normal life in both quality and duration. However, some forms of blindness affecting fer-rets may be hereditary and you should not breed a blind ferret.

Ferrets may also develop eye infections, usually manifested by watery eyes. A veterinarian can usually provide medication to treat the infection.

Blocked Scent Glands

If you purchase a de-scented baby, the anal scent glands were already removed. If your ferret has not been de-scented, you will need to check for the special problems that may ensue.

An unpleasant odor from your ferret that lasts only a few minutes is probably due to blocked anal scent glands. Although it is normal for a ferret to release these glands when it is very frightened or during the breeding sea-son, it is not normal for the animal to release them at any other time. De-scenting is recommended as standard practice for all ferrets.

If the ferret is releasing its scent glands when it shouldn't, it is time to visit the veterinarian. The veterinarian will probably evacuate the glands and administer an antibiotic because an infection is probably present. If this treatment does not clear up the prob-

Mites, Ticks, and Fleas

Mites: Mites sometimes take up residence in the ears of ferrets and other small animals. Mites cause the ears to itch and the ferret will become uncomfortable.

The easiest way to check for ear mites is to clean your pet's ears carefully. An accumulation of a black waxy substance in the ferret's ears can indicate ear mites. If the ferret's ears continue to generate black debris, you should ask your veterinarian to check the black substance under his microscope. It is not possible to accurately diagnose ear mites without this magnification.

You can pick up a cat-type ear mite medication from a pet store and follow the directions. The medication from the veterinarian or pet store contains an antibiotic that will treat any concurrent infection or help prevent one from starting as well as kill the ear mites.

Ticks: Ticks can attach to ferrets. The easiest treatment is to use a cat-approved antitick dip. (Dog dips are too strong.) You can find the dip at your local pet shop. Be sure to follow the directions carefully, especially concerning the amount of water to add as the dips are generally concentrated and require the addition of water. Make about a bucketful and dip the whole ferret in it.

Fleas: Little black specks on your ferret's skin indicate fleas. Dips are by far the easiest remedy. It is almost impossible to get a powder or spray all through a ferret's dense fur to the skin. Purchase a cat-type dip, follow the directions carefully, mix about a bucketful, and put the ferret in it.

You should also purchase a house and kennel spray. Use the spray on the carpet and cushions where the ferret tends to rest and play. Fleas and flea eggs will be living on these areas, just waiting for the ferret. Remember: do not use the spray on the ferret. Ask your veterinarian or pet store to recommend a combination of flea products that can safely be used together. There are many good flea "bombs" on the market now that kill the live fleas and have a second residual chemical to keep hatching flea eggs from developing into adult fleas. You must treat both the pet and the home environment to eliminate the problem.

Physical Injuries

Ferrets are small and agile and are quite frequently involved in accidents. Car doors, house doors, and being dropped while being carried are the main sources of injury.

Back Injuries: Many accidental injuries to ferrets occur to the spine. These injuries are always serious and should be seen by a veterinarian. Most may involve sprains, strains, or minor dislocations that respond well to extra warmth and rest. The veterinarian often prescribes drugs to relax the muscles and help the pet rest. Recovery may take from two weeks to two months. More serious injuries to the back may require surgery and a prolonged recovery period.

Broken Teeth: Broken teeth are uncommon in ferrets, but they can occur. Healthy teeth may be broken by an accident or by chewing on hard materials. Decayed teeth are the ones most often broken. Dry feed helps to keep the teeth clean and the gums massaged, thereby helping to prevent decay. If damage to teeth should occur, take your ferret to the veterinarian who will check for infection and, if necessary, clean the remaining teeth to prevent further problems. Your veterinarian will check you ferret's teeth as part of the yearly examination and will recommend cleaning if needed.

Foot Problems: Foot problems were once common among ferrets. In the 1800s ferrets were usually raised in cement- or clay-enclosed courtyards and were exposed to constantly wet or damp footing. This led to "foot rot," a common name for severe infection centered in the soft pads of the feet, and to other foot problems. Now that ferrets are raised and kept in wire cages or allowed free run of the house, foot rot and many other foot problems are almost nonexistent.

Bite Wounds: Ferrets are rough-and-tumble wrestlers for whom mock combat is a natural game. Sometimes play gets too rough and one animal accidentally bites and hurts another. There are usually no complications from this type of injury, although you should always be alert for any signs of infection. Occasionally, unneutered males become quite aggressive toward other ferrets and can cause injuries that require stitches. In such cases, clean the wounded area thoroughly and take the injured ferret to the veterinarian.

Surgery for Your Ferret

Ferrets tolerate surgery very well. Most problems arising from surgery are a result of delaying the decision for surgery until the ferret is weak. Problems also sometimes result from anesthesia.

Here are a few general guidelines to follow if your ferret needs surgery:

• If surgery is indicated, do it at once. Delay may cause the animal to become weaker and dehydrated. The problem also could become more severe as a result of delay.

• Do not give the ferret food or water before surgery. Follow your veterinarian's advice carefully. Your pet's life may depend on it.

• Avoid gas as an anesthesia if possible. Injectable drugs have shown much better results.

• Follow your veterinarian's advice for postoperative care at home.

• Keep the ferret warm during recovery. Loss of body temperature is a high-stress factor and can lead to setbacks in recovery and sometimes to death.

The most common surgeries performed on ferrets are:

Castration: This is the removal of the testes in males to prevent breeding and to reduce odor.

Spaying: This is the removal of the reproductive organs in females to prevent heat cycles.

Scent Gland Removal: This surgery is done to lessen odor or to remove glands that have recurrent infections.

Removal of tumors, lumps, etc.: This procedure is to remove abnormal growths that could be cancerous or that interfere with the activities of your pet. Ferrets appear most likely to acquire lymph system tumors. Chemotherapy is usually prescribed. Insulinomas, tumors of the pancreas, may be surgically removed.

Trauma repair: Surgery is indicated for the treatment of certain wounds to help them close more evenly and to promote healing.

Removal of intestinal blockages: This surgical procedure is life-saving to a ferret who has swallowed something which blocks the digestion and passing of food.

Spinal surgery: In the event of major damage to the spine, surgery can correct disk and joint problems in some cases.

Euthanasia

In the case of severe injury or debilitating illness, euthanasia becomes a painful choice. I know of no one who wants to put a loving pet to sleep, but continued suffering and pain with no hope of recovery sometimes makes this choice the right one.

Your veterinarian can use injectable drugs and certain gases to end the suffering of your pet, if necessary. Good health care, a proper diet, exercise, and care in handling can help avoid this painful choice.

Reproduction and Breeding

Because of the aplastic anemia problems in females, the odor and aggression problems in sexually intact males, and the low odds on kit survival, the decision to breed your ferrets should not be taken lightly. Breeding should *never* be undertaken in order to avoid the cost of spaying or as a whim. The pet owner must first accept the risks and responsibilities involved and think, "Yes, I understand I could lose my female, but this breeding is important to me."

Although the female is not frequently lost in breeding, it *can* happen. It is wiser to accept this at the beginning so that there are no surprises. You cannot change your mind halfway there.

Small- or Large-Scale Breeding?

Once you have decided that you do want to breed ferrets. you must decide on what scale and whether you are embarking on this endeavor for fun or for profit.

Large-scale breeding—colonies of 30 to 1000 females—requires substantial time and financial investment. Quality breeding stock should be purchased with great care. Cages, buildings, water systems, and customer acquisition plans should be well thought out ahead of time.

With large-scale breeding, you will no doubt plan to sell some of your kits to pet stores. It is important before you even start building your cages to contact the U.S. Department of Agriculture,

Animal, Plant, Health Inspection Service (A.P.H.I.S.). You must be licensed by them before you can sell even one kit to one pet store. Since they regulate your entire operation from caging to buildings to approved health plans, it is logical to contact them early to make sure your cages and buildings will meet their standards.

Small-scale breeding—just a few pet ferrets—is also a serious decision. You will have to decide whether to keep your own sexually intact stud or locate one you can send your females to. If the ferrets are inside, you have no guarantee that, when your females are in season, your male will also be in season. You will want to locate a backup stud just in case.

Check to make sure that your veterinarian will be available in case there are complications at whelping time. Your main time commitment comes when the kits are nearly ready to wean. You will want to devote the time to play with and love the babies so they are confident of people when they go to their new homes.

Unless you decide to keep all the young ferrets, you'll want to place classified ads under "Pets for Sale." You must be available to answer the many questions of a new ferret owner. When people come to look at the kits, you will need to educate them concerning ferret care and handling. It is the responsibility of the seller to see that the new owners have enough information to care for their ferrets properly. If you are not prepared to devote this time to help new ferret owners learn how to care for their pets, you should not bring unwanted kits into the world. Consult your veterinarian to arrange for spay/neutering before the kits are placed in their new homes. Spay/neutering and de-scenting costs are generally included in the purchase price of babies sold today.

We do not believe anyone can be successful in an animal-breeding venture if profit is the only motive. The real reason that making a profit is important is to have enough money for the animals' care and feed, and to enable you to continue doing what you love to do—raising animals. Unless you are independently wealthy, this makes profit necessary.

If you are just breeding a few ferrets, it is not as necessary to make a profit since most people can support this from the family budget. In the author's opinion, free or very inexpensive ferrets do no service to ferrets. Since we are against the idea of people acquiring animals on a whim and perhaps regretting it later we feel very strongly that the prospective customer must be willing to spend time to learn about the animal before purchasing it. We also feel that if customers must make a financial commitment to the animals before taking them home, they are more likely to be serious pet owners. Perhaps they will be quicker to seek veterinary care to protect their investments should this be necessary. Maybe they will be less likely to abandon an animal that they have paid good money to acquire.

Breeding One Pair

The easiest way to breed one pair of ferrets is to keep them outside year-round. They should be placed outside first in the summer so that later, as the seasons change, they can gradually become used to the cold weather. They will need a small, tight box packed with an insulating material such as straw. The reason ferrets are better left outside is that under natural conditions both will likely be in breeding season at the same time. The temperature and lights inside are confusing to their natural breeding cycles and you can easily end up with one animal in breeding condition and one not. In an outside setting, your ferrets will breed in the spring and kits will be born six weeks later.

Courtship and Mating

The female ferret is ready to breed when her vulva is fully swollen and

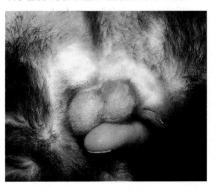

The male is ready to breed when the testicles are fully descended.

The female is ready to breed when the vulva is swollen.

56

there is a slight moisture discharge. The male is ready to breed when his testicles are fully descended and have developed to their full size.

When the female is placed in the male's cage, she will seem to reject his advances even though she is in season. This is perfectly natural. The male will be very aggressive with her. He will use his teeth to grab her behind the neck. When he has a good hold, she will become limp and passive. This allows the male to mate with the female. They may continue breeding for several hours.

While the female will likely lose some hair on her neck from the biting and holding, the male should not be so aggressive as to draw blood. While an aggressive hold is necessary, it is certainly not necessary to tolerate males who could injure a female.

While one mating is usually sufficient, we recommend leaving the male and female together for up to three days.

Pregnancy and Care During Pregnancy

After breeding, the female should be checked to make sure she has not developed any vaginal infections. If there is a colored discharge from the vulva, she must be taken to the veterinarian for appropriate therapy.

To be sure your female has ovulated and is starting out of estrus, check her one week to ten days after breeding to make sure the swelling of the vulva is reduced. While it may not be all the way back to normal size, the vulva should be much smaller than at breeding. If the vulva is the same size or larger, the female is not pregnant and not out of estrus. She must be rebred and then you must check the vulva size again one week to ten days after the second mating session.

Pregnancy lasts about six weeks. For the first three to four weeks, your female will not show any particular signs of pregnancy other than the

At mating time the male is aggressive and uses his teeth to grab the female behind the neck until she goes limp and is ready to mate.

reduction of the size of the vulva. The kits grow rapidly in her body during the last two weeks. She will become round and her stomach will feel full. She will sleep more than normal during the last week. She will be less active and may no longer want a roommate if you have a second ferret. It is best to place her wherever she is to have the kits at least one week before delivery. She will be much calmer at whelping time if she is in familiar surroundings.

Birth and Weaning Period

When your ferret has her kits, she may or may not want you near her. However, even if she prefers to handle the birth herself, you should peek in on her to see that all is going well. *Do not* bring people she is unfamiliar with into the whelping area. You will want her to stay as quiet and calm as possible.

Some females seem to really enjoy showing off the new family. I had one ferret friend, Crystal, who would lift her little hind leg to make sure we admired all her new babies. Other females are fiercely protective of their young. If your female is snappy when she has kits, it is not because she doesn't love you; it's just that right now, she's very concerned about her kits. She may be especially touchy the first few days after whelping and again after the first babies have been removed for weaning. However, she will be her usual cheerful self about one week after all the kits are weaned.

Kits are generally weaned by six weeks of age but some especially large kits can be weaned earlier. Small kits may need to wait a little longer. While the kits are still with the mother, it is helpful to keep a bowl of dry feed soaked with water in the cage. This way the kits become accustomed to the feed. This wet feed also keeps the mother from having to supply all the kits' needs. The same type feed should be fed to the weaned kits.

Health Risks to the Female

The highest risk to the female occurs at whelping. If the female becomes "glassy-eyed" and weak at delivery time, she will need to be seen by a veterinarian. If for some reason, she is unable to deliver her kits, she may have two kits who are trying to be born at the same time, or she may not have gone into strong enough contractions to expel the kits. Whatever the reason, she is in serious trouble and needs help.

Your veterinarian will probably have to perform a cesarean section (a C-section). We have never seen a female with serious delivery problems manage on her own. She will die if you do not contact a veterinarian. The C-section also carries risk to your female. The main problems with C-sections seem to be the anesthesia. An animal in debilitated, stressed condition who weighs only 1½ pounds (0.75 kg) is not the best candidate for surgery requiring anesthesia. There are no good choices at this point. It will help if the lightest possible anesthetic dose is used.

After surgery the ferret should be placed on a towel or a heating pad turned to low to help her maintain her body temperature. While it is likely she will not be able to care for her kits, they can be removed from their sacs and placed on the heating pad with the mother. The kits will not be very wiggly at first, for when the mother was anesthetized, they were also. All you can do is wait and hope from this point.

Another risk to your female is mastitis. Mastitis is an infection of the milk glands. Check for mastitis by picking the female up and feeling the areas around the teats—they should be soft. Even when the kits are two or three weeks old and the mother is producing considerable amounts of milk, this area should be soft. If this area is hard, the ferret must go to the veterinarian to be placed on antibiotics. If left untreated, the infection can spread through her body and become life-threatening. There is a good likelihood she will lose the kits at this point.

Raising and Socializing the Young

Pick up your kits often starting at three weeks of age. Even with their eyes closed, they become used to you and start to relate to you. When the kits are weaned and eating well, play with the babies. Now is the time for them to learn to expect a Linatone treat now and then. They will enjoy being carried and stroked.

Reread "Adjusting to the New Home and General Care." This is your guide to socializing those kits. *Do not* simply place them in another cage and ignore them until someone takes them home. You will play a large part in determining how they will feel about people in the future.

A ferret family. Some females want to display their kits; others are very protective.

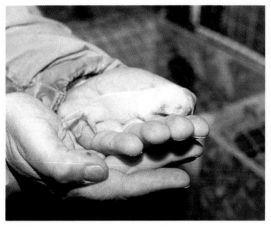
One-week-old kits are blind and utterly helpless.

Two-week-old kits nursing avidly.

Three-week-old kits nestling close to their mother.

A mother with her own four-week-old kits and a two-week-old foster kit (right).

A mother with a litter of four-week-old kits.

Weaned kits at six and one-half weeks of age.

Understanding Ferrets

History of Ferrets

Ferrets are members of the Mustelidae family. Other members of this diverse family are the weasel, mink, otter, sable, badger, and skunk. The scientific name of the domestic ferret is *Mustela furo.* There is some disagreement as to who the ferrets' wild ancestors were. Scientific evidence points to two possible choices. The steppe polecat *(Mustela eversmanni)* found in Siberia, or the European polecat *(Mustela putorius) are* both considered possible ancestors.

There is a wild animal found in the United States that is referred to as a "ferret." This is the black-footed ferret whose scientific name is *Mustela nigripes.* This animal, which is on the endangered species list, is not even considered a possible ancestor of the domestic ferret. While sable domestic ferrets have black

Members of the family Mustelidae. From top to bottom: otter, ranch mink, skunk, ferret, ermine (winter coat), and weasel.

feet, they are not closely related to the rare black-footed ferret.

The native American black-footed ferret, *Mustela nigripes,* was listed as an endangered mammal in North America in 1967. By the mid-1970s, many feared them extinct. Because of the devotion and work of many people, the black-footed ferrets were successfully reproduced in captivity for the first time by Dr. Donald R. Kwitkowski of the Wyoming Game and Fish Department at the Sybille Research Unit in Wyoming. The domestic ferrets were used to perfect some of the reproduction techniques used on the black-footed ferrets. Thank goodness these beautiful species of ferrets, while still endangered, have now been successfully reproduced. Our domestic ferrets were glad to be able to lend a hand to their beautiful wild cousins.

Ferrets were first domesticated by the Egyptians in 3000 B.C. Most historians believe that the Crusaders of the 10th to 12th centuries introduced the working ferret to Europe. These domestic ferrets may have bred with the common European polecat. The European polecat, the steppe polecat, and the domestic ferret are so closely related that they can be crossbred in the manner of dogs and wolves. It is interesting to note that the offspring resulting from such crosses tend to resemble the more aggressive parent and thus do not make good pets.

Make sure your pet ferret came from a reputable source and that it was born and raised in the United States. Some foreign countries use the wild species of ferrets for fur, and these are not domestic animals. This would be the equivalent of obtaining a wolf when you thought you were acquiring a German shepherd or a Siberian husky.

Ferrets have been in the United States for over 300 years. They were used in the 1800s for rodent control. The "ferretmeister" would come with his ferrets to a farm or grainery and release his ferrets. These working ferrets ran into the holes and hiding places of the rodents and the rats ran out. The people would wait outside with shovels and terrier-type dogs and kill as many rodents as they could. Ferrets are sometimes kept on small farms and at feed mills for rodent control. The normal range of a ferret in these circumstances is about 200 meters from the place it considers home. Ferrets traveling through rat tunnels leave trace odors that trigger fear in rats and mice, causing them to flee. There are also some dangers for the ferrets: they may become trapped in a rat tunnel. Anytime you allow your pet outside, it could become injured. Be sure all your ferrets' vaccinations are current, including its rabies vaccinations.

Ferrets have also been used successfully to help wire planes in hard-to-reach places. Since ferrets love to enter anything that looks like a tunnel, it is a simple matter to attach a wire and have them run down a tunnel and return.

Ferrets have also been used in scientific research. Since they catch the same "common cold" as humans, they have been used in medical investigations.

Ferrets have steadily increased in popularity since the 1970s. Initially, ferrets were prized only for their abilities as ratters. As more information was made available and more people learned about ferrets, their popularity skyrocketed.

Today, there are veterinarians who specialize in ferrets. There are catalogs

The black-footed American ferret (Mustela nigripes), *at right, is not an ancestor of the domestic ferret, at left.*

filled with ferret toys and products. There are ferret clubs in nearly any area that you live. There are at least two national ferret organizations promoting ferret health and ferret ownership. There are ferret shows that are both educational and enjoyable. Ferrets compete in conformation and color classes as well as costume classes. Fun-type classes are also held for digging, yawning, and hopping events.

Ferrets as Predatory Animals

Ferrets used to be much better predatory animals than they are today. Because they are kept primarily as pets, responsible breeders have bred only very docile adults. Many ferrets have become so gentle that we hear more and more stories of ferrets being very casual about rodents. The owners of a pet store once told me that they had a mouse escape and hide out in the ferret cage. The pet male ferret yawned and finished his nap.

The ferret head is oval-shaped with bright, expressive eyes.

The unfortunate mouse then ventured into the next cage of ferrets and found a female who still had some hunting instincts left.

We know of another family who has one of the male ferrets we bred. This ferret has been completely adopted by their parakeet. The parakeet regurgitates food for him and regularly enters the ferret's cage. The parakeet pecks the ferret and initiates chase games. This ferret clearly has little hunting instinct left.

My tip: Friendships between animals that could become predators should always be supervised for the animals' safety.

Common Misconceptions About Ferrets

The most common misconception is that ferrets are European polecats bred in captivity—wild animals. As we have seen in the preceding section, this simply is not true.

Another misconception is that ferrets will establish in the wild. Ferrets have been in the United States in large numbers for over 300 years and have never been able to do this. There are no wild ferret colonies anywhere in the world. Errors probably stem from confusing the domestic ferret *(Mustela furo)* with the American black-footed ferret *(Mustela nigripes)*.

Still another misconception is that ferrets who get loose will destroy thousands of rabbits. Many years ago (and even today in England) ferrets were sometimes used to hunt rabbits. This is because ferrets could enter rabbit holes at one end and the frightened rabbits would exit at the other end. Ferrets never could catch many rabbits. Hunters would wait at the exit holes and get the rabbits as they ran

The neck is short, the body muscular and lean, the fur dense and soft.

out. Today, this practice is illegal in the United States.

External Features

Ferrets are small furry creatures. Adult males are usually about 16 inches (40 cm) long and weigh from 3 to 5 pounds (1.5 to 2.5 kg). Females are smaller, about 14 inches (35 cm) long and about 1½ to 3 pounds (0.75 to 1.5 kg).

The ferret head is rather oval-shaped; in males the head is usually broader and less pointed than in females. The eyes are bright, clear, and expressive. Ferrets see well in dim light. They do not see well in bright light and they cannot discriminate colors. They can, however, be trained to discriminate objects, and according to at least one scientific report, rank near primates in object discrimination tests.

Ferrets have a total of 40 teeth. On each side there are three incisors on the top and three on the bottom, two canine teeth on the top and two on the bottom, four premolar teeth on the top and three on the bottom, and one molar top and two on the bottom.

The ferret neck is typically short; the body elongated, lean, muscular, and athletic looking. The legs are short. The feet have five toes, all ending in claws. At the bottom of the feet are many tiny pads. These tiny pads may be sensitive to vibrations and help the ferret locate prey and other objects.

The body fur is dense and soft. The underlying skin is smooth. Ferrets have poorly developed sweat glands in the skin and cannot tolerate temperatures above (95°F (35°C). If you leave your ferret outside in the summer, be sure that it does not stay in

Skull of a ferret showing teeth arrangement.

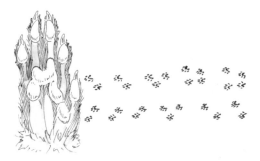

Underside of the foot of a ferret and footprints.

direct sunlight and that there are some shady spots available to it.

Internal Anatomy

Ferrets are so flexible that people sometimes wonder if they have bones. Yes, they do—just as all vertebrates. Ferrets have a long vertebral column, or backbone, made up of 7 cervical, or neck, vertebrae; 15 thoracic, or chest vertebrae; 5 lumbar and 3 sacral vertebrae in the lower back region; and 18 caudal vertebrae in the tail. They also have 15 pairs of ribs, which you can easily feel on the front upper part of your ferret's body. They also have the other skeletal features typical of vertebrates.

The circulatory system of a ferret is unusual in one respect—there is only a single central artery in the neck. Some zoologists believe that this midline vessel allows continued blood flow to the brain when the ferret turns its head a full 180°—as is its habit, especially when it ventures into small tight places as it is prone to do. (Such head turning would squeeze a lateral blood vessel and lead to impaired blood flow to the brain.)

The spleen of ferrets is usually much larger than what would be expected in an animal of this size. This sometimes leads veterinarians unfamiliar with ferrets to diagnose an enlarged spleen, and this can confuse a correct diagnosis.

The part of the neck just below the skull appears to play an important part in the psychosexual system of ferrets. A mother ferret carries her kits by the skin at the back of the neck and the kits become quiet and limp. This behavioral. pattern may have developed in the ferret's ancestors as a way of lessening danger when a mother is moving her kits away from predators or to a new den. Later, during adolescence, young ferrets—ages 3 to 7 months—induce this limp and submissive state in others during mock combat, sexual play, and attempts at dominance. As adults the male grabs the female by the back neck area to force her to submit to mating.

Intelligence and Sense Organs

Ferrets do not have very well developed sight. They do, however, have keen senses of hearing, smell, and touch. These senses are, in fact, developed enough so that a blind ferret can cope nearly as well as a sighted ferret. A blind ferret will sniff out and explore its surroundings very thoroughly—more thoroughly than a sighted ferret. Once familiar with its area. it will hop, jump, run, and play much as a sighted ferret does.

Ferrets are thought to be intelligent animals, probably similar to dogs in their intelligence level. Their curiosity, play behavior, and trainability make their intelligence readily apparent.

Because ferrets are interested in everything, they can be difficult to train.

You are competing with a multitude of things for their undivided attention.

My tip: Short training sessions are best; otherwise, the ferret will become bored.

Social Behavior and Play Gestures

A single ferret will amuse itself with games and toys. If there is another pet in the home, the ferret will make every attempt to teach it ferret games; ferrets are very social animals.

When a new ferret is introduced, ferrets will engage in hopping, jumping, clucking, and neck grabbing to establish a pecking order. The dominant ferret will drag the more submissive ferret around by the back of the neck, much as a mother carries her kits. Once this matter is settled, they can get down to the serious business of play. My mother keeps two of her ferrets in one cage and another in a single cage. When the two are released for play time, they climb up the second cage and cluck for their other buddy to be released to play.

Ferrets like to sleep curled up together, much as you would expect to find a pile of puppies who are in the same litter. If you have four ferrets who know each other and a huge cage, all four will sleep in one crowded pile.

Mock combat and chase are the two most popular ferret games. Mock combat is very similar to the gestures of kittens. The ferret wants you to tap your hand on the ground bouncing toward it and away from it. The chase game is often initiated by a tug on the pants. You chase it—it chases you.

Tug-of-war can be initiated with a washcloth. Drag it along the ground and let the ferret "steal" it. When you take hold again, the ferret will pull and attempt to steal it back.

HOW-TO:
Understanding Your Pet

Hopping, jumping and bounding towards you are normal ferret play gestures.

Body Language

As you get to know your ferret you will come to associate certain stances and movements with your ferret's mood. Is it happy? Fearful? You can often tell by how it moves and acts— its body language.

Hopping, jumping, and bouncing toward you: People sometimes believe the ferret is "after" them. We have even heard of people who thought the caged ferret was "lunging at the wires" for them. Actually, the ferret is trying to entice you to play. The gesture is similar in looks to the gleeful abandon with which some kittens jump and play. The back is arched and the ferret frequently clucks at the same time.

Running backward: This happens sometimes as you go to pick up the ferret. It is either unsure of you or not too sure it wants to be picked up just now.

Puffing: The ferret sits on all four feet, back slightly arched, and raises all the hair until it stands straight out. Even the tail hairs stand away from the body. If two ferrets have been in a tiff, the loser does this. The ferret is

trying to seem larger than it really is. This is a fear gesture.

Teeth on your hand when holding: Your ferret is asking to get down or telling someone, "Be careful, big person. I'm bigger than I look!" The best course of action is to tell the ferret. "No!" or "Careful," and continue holding it. We don't want to teach it that this is the way to get down.

Swings head quickly to smell hand when picked up: Ferrets don't see particularly well. When a giant picks up a ferret, it wants to inspect the giant more closely.

Sound Language

Ferrets make several types of noises that, like body stances and movements, you can learn to identify and understand.

Clucking: Ranges from a soft "cluck," "cluck" to a "dook," "dook" noise. We have seen ferrets do this when they are very happy and also when they are angry. This seems to be an all-

purpose noise depending on the situation. When angry or excited, the noise seems a little higher pitched and more rapid.

Hissing: This is more of a fear noise than an aggression noise.

A ferret that is unsure of itself (or of you) may run backward for a few steps.

Soft words and reassurance are called for in most cases.

Screaming: A ferret who is accidentally stepped on or terrified can scream. It sounds almost like a child who throws its head back and screams, "Ahhhh!" This will certainly get you to jump quickly off its tail if that's the problem. Soft words and reassurances are definitely needed here. This is not the time to yell at it.

When a ferret is puffing, all of its fur stands on end.

A Word About Regulations

Most states have always grouped ferrets with other pets such as dogs and cats and have never established separate regulations governing the keeping of ferrets. Other states once had laws specifically regulating ferrets but have changed these laws in the light of scientific evidence. A few states, however, still do classify ferrets separately from other common domestic pets and have specific laws concerning ferrets. Such separate government regulations stem from misconceptions about ferrets and antiquated laws based on these misconceptions.

At one time, the idea that ferrets were wild animals that could establish in the wild was widely held. At that time, laws prohibiting or severely restricting ferrets were passed in many areas. Since then interested people have presented the facts to state legislatures and in virtually all cases the laws have been changed.

In the past, for example, a few states expressed concern over any possible rabies problems with ferrets. However, even before there was a vaccine approved specifically for ferrets, there were very few documented cases of ferrets with rabies. There is now an approved rabies vaccine for ferrets, so of course, this is an obsolete objection.

Let's take a brief look at how laws were changed in a few states, starting with Pennsylvania, the state we live in.

When we first began raising ferrets in Pennsylvania, breeders and anyone who sold even one ferret had to purchase a $50 per year license from the Pennsylvania Game Commission. Anyone wanting to purchase a pet ferret had to obtain a $10 per year license from the Game Commission before they could take possession of the ferret. There were no set guidelines concerning the circumstances under which applications for licenses would be accepted or rejected, and it could take from one week to several months to receive a license. If you moved with your pet ferret from another state into Pennsylvania, you might not know that ferrets were under the control of the Pennsylvania Game Commission and if you were "found out" your pet could be confiscated and killed. This situation was in many ways bizarre, and the Game Commission was expending considerable money and personnel to regulate ferrets—money and personnel that could have been used on other animal concerns.

To try to change this situation, we went to a local state representative who was on the Fish and Game Commission. We presented him with all the information we had gathered showing that ferrets are domestic animals not able to establish in the wild. We then testified at legislative committee meetings. The result was that a new law was passed that removed ferrets from Game Commission regulation. Pennsylvania now treats ferrets like any other domestic animals.

We have discussed this situation in detail to make the point that antiquated laws can be changed—if concerned citizens gather the scientific data and present it to the proper authorities.

A brief look at action in a few states substantiates this point. At one time West Virginia did not allow ferrets under any circumstances. West

Virginia residents often crossed into Maryland to buy a ferret and then illegally took it back to their home state. When a group of concerned citizens presented the scientific facts to the West Virginia lawmakers, the restrictions were lifted. A similar situation occurred in Maine. Now both West Virginia and Maine treat ferrets just like any other domestic pet.

Alaska presents an interesting case. Alaska laws used to permit ferrets. Then, the Alaska Game Commission, operating under false assumptions about the animals, issued regulations that, in effect, said "No more ferrets." It was not a law, but an interpretation by the Game Commission that ferrets fell under wildlife rules. After a few years the Commission confiscated the ferrets of a dedicated ferret pet owner. He presented scientific information showing that ferrets were domestic animals to the Alaska Fish and Wildlife Commission but the regulations were not changed. Frustrated, the pet owner took the case to court. Over 400 scientific references were produced showing that ferrets are domestic animals—not wild—and the judge removed the ferrets from wildlife regulations.

There are, however, a few states that still have laws restricting ferrets. Among these states are California, Hawaii, Massachusetts, Michigan, and South Carolina. In most of these states, efforts are under way to examine the scientific literature and adjust the laws. There are also a few cities that have local regulations. For example, there are some boroughs in New York City that still view ferrets as illegal pets. Contacting your local pet stores to obtain the names of a nearby ferret organization is a good place to start if you live in or move to an area with ferret regulations. They can put you in touch with people working on presenting current scientific data to modify these regulations.

Useful Literature and Addresses

Useful Addresses

American Ferret Association, Inc. (AFA)
P.O. Box 3986
Frederick, Maryland 21705
Shows, clubs, general and health information, supplies, newsletter

United Ferret Organization (UFO)
P.O. Box 606
Assonet, Massachusetts 02702
Shows, clubs, general and health information, supplies, newsletter

Ferret World
6 Water Street
Box 555
Assonet, Massachusetts 02702
Color catalogue of ferret supplies, ferret food

Path Valley Farm, Inc.
P.O. Box 233
Willow Hill, Pennsylvania 17271
Ferret information, ferret food, supplies

Useful Literature

Biology & Diseases of the Ferret, James G. Fox, D.V.M. Lea & Febiger, Philadelphia, 1988.
The standard work on the subject, this volume is intended primarily for veterinarians.

Index

All inquiries should be addressed to:
Barron's Educational Series, Inc.
250 Wireless Boulevard
Hauppauge, New York 11788

International Standard Book No. 0-8120-9021-7

Library of Congress Catalog No. 94-37728

Library of Congress Cataloging-in-Publication Data

Morton, E. Lynn.
    Ferrets : everything about purchase, care, nutrition, diseases, behavior, and breeding / E. Lynn (Fox) and Chuck Morton ; consulting editor, Matthew M. Vriends. —2nd ed., rev.
        p. cm.
    Chuck Morton's name appears first on the earliest edition.
    Includes bibliographical references (p.   ) and index.
    ISBN 0-8120-9021-7
    1. Ferrets as pets. I. Morton, Chuck. II. Vriends, Matthew M., 1937– . III. Title.
SF459.F47M67   1995
636'.97447—dc20   94-37728
                                                                    CIP

Printed and Bound in Hong Kong

5678   9955   9876543

Note of Warning

This book deals with the keeping and care of ferrets as pets. In working with animals, you may occasionally sustain scratches or bites. Have such wounds treated by a doctor at once.

Ferrets, like all animals, can have external parasites, some of which can be transmitted to humans or other pets. Always check with your veterinarian if you suspect problems. When acquiring any new pet, an early medical examination is a good investment.

Ferrets must be watched very carefully during the necessary and regular exercise period in the house. To avoid life-threatening accidents, be particularly careful that your pet does not gnaw on any electrical wires.

Ferrets, like all other pets, must be watched carefully when they are near infants. Caution is required at all times—both when children are sleeping and when they are awake. The only completely safe pet for a young child is a teddy bear.

About the Author

E. Lynn "Fox" Morton, received her teaching degree in Special Education. Her love for animals led her to devote her full time efforts to the raising of ferrets and purebred cats. She currently raises ferrets in a small mountain valley in south central Pennsylvania. She has also co-authored several articles in conjunction with the National Zoological Park, Smithsonian Institution, Washington, D.C.

Photo Credits

Aaron Norman: Front cover, pages 20, 29, 40, 64, 65; Judith Strom: pages 33 (bottom), 44; all other photos were provided by Path Valley Farm.